Child Advocacy

Child Advocacy

History, Theory, and Practice

James R. Tompkins
APPALACHIAN STATE UNIVERSITY
BOONE, NORTH CAROLINA

Benjamin L. Brooks
BELMONT ABBEY COLLEGE
BELMONT ABBEY, NORTH CAROLINA

Timothy J. Tompkins
COMMUNITY RELATIONS MANAGER
CITYSEARCH.COM
MORRISVILLE, NORTH CAROLINA

CAROLINA ACADEMIC PRESS
Durham, North Carolina

Library of Congress Cataloging-in-Publication Data

Tompkins, James R. 1935–
    Child Advocacy : history, theory, and practice / James R.
Tompkins, Benjamin L. Brooks, Timothy J. Tompkins.
        p.   cm.
    Includes bibliographical references.
    ISBN 0-89089-959-2
    1. Child welfare—United States. 2. Children's rights—United
States. 3. Children—Services for—United States. 4. Social
advocacy—United States. I. Brooks, Benjamin L. (Benjamin
Leigh), 1945–   . II. Tompkins, Timothy J., 1964–   .
III. Title.
    HV741.T65   1998
    362.7'0973—DC21   98-5102
                                                             CIP

Carolina Academic Press
700 Kent Street
Durham, North Carolina 27701
Telephone (919) 489-7486
Fax (919) 493-5668
www.cap-press.com

Printed in the United States of America

*This book is dedicated to all children
and especially those in our families.*

Contents

Preface

Advocacy Overview

One fundamental crisis in American life has to do with the way we raise our children and provide for their general welfare. Children with special needs or those experiencing disabilities go unserved, undereducated, or inadequately educated. Mental health and correctional facilities are filled with disaffected neglected children. While significant attempts have been made to get services to families in crisis, family disorganization as indicated by increasing deviance rates is a continuing major concern of those looking at basic child environments. Child abuse remains a major social problem. Juvenile delinquency continues to increase. Many children are not attending school for one reason or another, some too complex to comprehend. The United States has the worst record for infant deaths due to brain injury, postnatal asphyxia, and so forth. We do not have an adequate public health program that makes health care effectively available to children, especially to the poor. Many children continue to suffer from malnutrition, do not receive food during the day while they are in school, and do not have even minimal medical and dental services.

Part of the problem is our failure as a society to effectively deliver necessary resources to children through out primary institutions (family and school). It is reasonable to conclude that our large and awkward social and physical structures established to serve children have become part of the problem for children. It would appear, then:

- The person who has ecologically relevant different behavior is stigmatized for the difference.
- Decisions made about him/her are primarily based on group maintenance in contrast to child development criteria.
- The child has no *Advocate* to represent his/her interest and is therefore vulnerable.
- Stigmatizing involves moral and ethical issues.

There are many manifestations of child advocacy and many different frameworks in which it can be viewed. First, it must be said that child advocacy is an emerging social movement with increasing significance for the public and the professional and political communities. Child advocacy is becoming an important aspect of the general registration of concern for the welfare and human rights of children. *For the purpose of this text child advocacy will be view as a process that seeks to champion the rights of all children and to make every child's needs known and met.* In a sense, child advocacy can be characterized as representing the personal and practical needs and requirements of children where/when the children and their natural advocates cannot ably represent themselves in fulfillment of those personal and practical needs. Individuals, citizen groups, professional groups, and especially educators with alliances of all these groups can assume advocacy roles for children's needs and requirements.

J.R.T., Boone, NC
B.L.B., Belmont Abbey, NC
T.J.T., Morrisville, NC

Child Advocacy

Chapter 1

Introduction: Advocacy Overview

This text on child advocacy is directed at analyzing the alienation of children from supportive environments that are vital to children's psychological and social development. Alienation is a complex multiform problem. It includes:

- the absence of supportive home and school environments which usually involves the presence of abusive and generally growth negating influences;

- the absence of needed special resources required by some children for satisfactory adaptation, such as a personally and technically resourceful adult;

- the absence of professional services provided by community agencies but not effectively available to children; and,

- the presence of subtle but powerful forces in the environment to alienate the child, such as a superficially considered psychometric process that "identifies" the child as having significant negative differences or other distinctions, labels the child, and then fails to provide a better environment.

Child advocacy is an emerging social movement with increasing significance for the public, professional, and political communities. Child advocacy is becoming an important aspect of the general registration of concern for the welfare and human rights of children. Child advocacy is viewed as a process that seeks to champion the rights of all children and to make every child's needs known and met. In a sense, child advocacy can be characterized as representing the personal and practical needs and requirements of children where/when the children and their natural advocates cannot ably represent themselves in fulfillment of those personal and practical needs. Individuals, citizen groups, professional groups, and especially educators with alliances between/among all of these groups can assume advocacy roles for children's needs and requirements.

One fundamental crisis in American life has to do with the way we raise our children and provide for their general welfare. Historically, children with special needs or those experiencing disabilities have gone unserved, undereducated, or inadequately served. Thus mental health and correctional facilities are filled with disaffected children. While significant attempts have been made to provide services to families in crisis, family disorganization, as indicated by increasing deviance rates, continues to be a major concern of those looking at basic child environments. Child abuse remains a major social problem. Juvenile delinquency continues to increase. Many children are not attending school for one reason or another, some too complex to comprehend. The United States has the worst record for infant deaths due to brain injury and postnatal asphyxia. Even today, in the closing of the twentieth century, we do not have an adequate public health program that makes health care effectively available to children, especially to the poor. Many children continue to suffer from malnutrition, do not receive food during the school day, and do not have minimal medical and dental services.

Part of the problem is our failure as a society to effectively mediate necessary resources to children throughout primary institutions (family and school). It seems reasonable to wonder how much our large and awkward social and physical structures established to serve children have become part of the problem. It would appear that the child who has ecologically relevant different behavior is stigmatized for the difference and decisions made about him/her are primarily based on group maintenance in contrast to child development criteria. These children have no *Advocate* to represent their interest and are therefore vulnerable for stigmatizing which involves both moral and ethical issues.

There are many manifestations of child advocacy and many different frameworks in which it can be viewed. First, it must be said that child advocacy is an emerging social movement with increasing significance for the public, professional, and political communities. Child advocacy is becoming an important aspect of the general registration of concern for the welfare, and human rights of children. For the purpose of this text, advocacy will be viewed as a process that seeks to champion the rights of all children and to make every child's needs known and met. In a sense, child advocacy can be characterized as representing the personal and practical needs and requirements of children where/when the children and their natural advocates cannot ably represent themselves in fulfillment of those personal and practical needs. Individuals, citizen groups, professional groups, and especially educators with alliances of all must assume advocacy roles for children's needs and requirements if it is expected to change the current status of the child. Advocacy for disaffected and special needs children depends upon the collaboration of those adults most responsible for children's betterment and advancement. It includes the interagency efforts and the support of all community child-serving systems, and especially parents.

Chapter Two

The Emergence of Child Advocacy at the National Level

The advocacy movement, which emerged in the late sixties to dramatize the needs of children and youth, appeared to be conceptually related to but independent of other social movements (civil rights action, women's liberation, and consumer protection). This advocacy movement provided one of the first opportunities for civic and professional organizations across the country to voice concerns, problems, needs, and aspirations of their constituents. Within this service delivery system personnel became more intent upon and even militant about expanding the national consciousness with regard to the needs of the ill, disabled, and the handicapped populations in institutional and community settings. Visibility was viewed as an important catalyst for obtaining the financial, administrative, and legislative support required to improve service delivery and/or existing conditions.

It appears appropriate and highly advisable at the turn of the twentieth century that communities and service professions become acquainted with the achievements and the on-going programs within the child advocacy movement in order to effectively formulate strategies to achieve future change. It is in light of the increasing concern for the needs of all people that the contemporary child advocacy movement is discussed. The principles, values, concerns, and processes of child advocacy are neither alien nor inappropriate to the work of the public, professional, and political communities. Indeed, the continued theme throughout this text will echo that individuals, citizen groups, professional groups, and especially educators with alliances between and within all of these groups can assume roles for meeting the children's needs and requirements.

The Joint Commission on Mental Health of Children (JCMHC), which represented the interests of child health, education, and development, stimulated national interest in child advocacy through its report that was published in 1970. The report entitled, *Crisis in child mental health: Challenge for the 1970's,* was in the beginning received with mixed emotions. However, following intense study within the U.S. Department of Health, Education and Welfare (HEW), considerable activity was generated to respond to the concerns and issues raised by those who sought to protect the rights and promote the interests of their young constituents.

Crisis in child mental health: Challenge for the 1970's (JCMHC, 1970) was submitted to Congress and addressed several issues relating to child advocacy. The report stated that the focus of child advocacy in the community should be upon the development of commitment by various community groups to the concept of advocacy and acceptance of precise roles as a result of that commitment. The report also recommended that states produce a child advocacy plan that would conform to relevant federal legislation. If the State Plan did not conform, funds would not be available to that state to participate in the program. In addition, the report suggested that within a geographic area there be existing service delivery systems mandated by legislation to ensure that children have access to and receive service(s) they need. However, not all children in need were being served. The report stated that child advocacy systems should connect children outside the delivery system with the service providers, who would then assume responsibility among themselves to continue these services on a cooperative and coordinated basis. Federal-State-Local interface would enable these sectors to operate as part of one delivery system. However, at this point in the advocacy movement most agencies and their delivery systems needed to become better organized to pursue the development of child advocacy programs. In addition, there was a need for an agency outside the cooperating agencies to hold the service providers accountable to all children.

During the 1960s and early 1970s, Dr. Reginald Lourie, then Director of Psychiatric Services for Children at Children's Hospital (Washington, DC), and his brother Normal Lourie, with the Pennsylvania Department of Social Services, led the effort to keep the Commission's recommendations on child advocacy alive and visible within the Health, Education and Welfare (HEW) offices. This effort was also implemented within the national and federal professional offices in the metropolitan Washington area.

In 1970 at a meeting with Health, Education and Welfare Office of Child Development personnel, Norman Lourie stated that money was not the central issue in the development and implementation of child advocacy programs; financial support could conceivably cause difficulties. For example, if a federal or state agency were to provide funds to one community agency to create or improve a service but not allocate funds to similar agencies, the unsupported agencies might be alienated and cause a break in the advocacy role the community purported to establish. Therefore, as a general rule it was recommended that funds from existing programs be utilized to support advocacy (Lourie, 1972).

Lourie (1972) suggested that federal and state agencies view child advocacy as the process of developing facilitating structures to connect children and child-serving agencies. In turn the agencies would assume responsibility among themselves to develop structures on a planned coordinated basis. The implementation of this approach would ultimately assure that all children in need would receive maximum attention from available resources. Once the broad national-state framework was established, the local thrust would be to obtain commitment to the goals of child advocacy from community groups and agencies serving children. They, too, would embark upon a coordinated service delivery pattern with specific responsibilities (Lourie, 1972).

The implementation of this approach would ultimately assure that all children in need would receive maximum attention from available resources. Once the broad national-state framework was established, the local (community) thrust would be to obtain commitment to the goals of child advocacy from community groups and agencies serving children. They, too, would embark upon a coordinated service delivery pattern with specific responsibilities (Lourie, 1972).

However, community power structures were suspect of child advocacy mainly because it might have meant sacrificing what they saw as important policies, procedures, and resources. Often, politicians did not wish to identify with or support child advocacy because national, state, and local legislation did not provide an adequate mechanism for implementing child advocacy strategies at this point in time. Before state governors and city mayors would be secure and willing to support child advocacy, laws needed to be changed. All legislation dealing with human service delivery to children and youth needed to be amended to increase the benefits to this group and support the development and implementation of child advocacy. Since there was (and still is) little legislation to support coordinated activities for children, federal and state agencies needed to agree upon and affirm the concept of child advocacy and establish pilot programs to precede the development of legislation (JCMHC, 1970).

In February 1971, Wolf Wolfensberger, an eminent Canadian child psychologist and advocate, presented his perspective of advocacy to a small group of JCMHC and HEW representatives. Wolfensberger, (1971c) described two types of relationships that people maintain or exercise with each other—*instrumental* and *expressive*. *Instrumental functions* relate to the practical problems of everyday life and are generally of a problem-solving or task-oriented nature. *Expressive functions* involve mutual affection between people and reflect and meet deep-seated and essential emotional needs. *Advocacy* involves the determination of a child's (or children's) instrumental and expressive needs and the development of strategies to meet them. Advocacy might imply the assumption of an expressive function with deep emotional commitment and/or the assumption of an instrumental function to work out a problem of life or living. This distinction between expressive and instrumental relationships is an important one since the relationship generally maintained between systems and institutionalized children can be characterized as primarily instrumental; expressive needs are, therefore, often unmet. Wolfensberger (1971c) defined citizen advocacy as:

> ...a mature, competent citizen representing, as if they were his own, the interests of another citizen who is impaired in his instrumental competency, or who has Major expressive needs which are unmet and which are likely to remain unmet without special intervention.

The mandate of the advocate, therefore, is to use culturally appropriate means to meet the instrumental and expressive needs of the impaired person. Advocacy should be pursued in a manner which minimizes conflicts involving the advocate, the person assisted, and the individuals or agencies involved. It should not be exercised by agencies or persons acting in professional roles; the most desirable advocates are competent citizens, free of vested interests. Wolfensberger indicated there are several forms of advocacy:

- *Generic*—wherein an individual serves as an advocate for an entire category of people (e.g., the handicapped).

- *Corporate*—wherein a group with some legal and/or professional identity (e.g., National Recreation and Park Association) serves as an advocate for an entire category of people and a certain type of service.
- *Dispersed*—wherein several people share advocacy functions and responsibilities for one person.
- *Multiple*—wherein an individual, family, and small group advocates for more than one person.
- *Crisis*—wherein an individual or group assists a person who needs immediate and extensive time and attention in a crisis situation.
- *Youth*—wherein a mature youth assumes an advocacy role for another youth in need of assistance. (Wolfensberger, 1976).

During this same time period in the early seventies Tracey and Gibbins (1971) presented a paper at the White House Conference on Children. In their presentation they indicated that child advocacy emerges from the position that services directed to children are really oriented toward (or reflect the interests of) the child-serving agency itself. This means that services ostensibly provided for the good of children are actually planned for the good of the agency to promote or expand a particular professional bias or to obtain funding. The paper further suggested that programs are offered to avoid or evade a problem; personnel label a child and isolate him or her in institutions or refer him/her to other agencies without significantly providing assistance. Accordingly then, advocacy should revolve around service delivery systems most closely related to children—medical, social-welfare, education, and legal-correctional. Child advocacy action should relate to the systems and their structures (neighborhood, city, state, etc.) and form a thread that unites all child-serving agencies at all structural levels (Tracey & Gibbins, 1971).

Child advocacy was presented in terms of functions and the ways in which control is maintained over the outcomes of children's programs. For example, advocacy may serve an adversary function when there is direct confrontation with policies, procedures, and people that impede the maximum growth and development of children. There is also the policy-influencing function that attempts to change attitudes, philosophies, policies, and procedures within a service agency to create greater responsiveness to children's needs. Advocacy models (adversary, influential, etc.) might adopt certain approaches to distributing and maintaining control by one of the following:

- utilization of existing professional sources;
- redistribution of responsibility and authority within or between agencies; and,
- establishment of a new authority external to the agencies (Tracey & Gibbins, 1971).

Just prior to the JCMHC report and the position papers of Wolfenberger and Tracey & Gibbins, the U.S. Office of Education for the Handicapped-National Institute for Mental Health (BEH-NIMH) Committee, during the summer of 1969, began an effort to develop an improved method for meeting the needs of emotionally disturbed children both in the home and the community. As in earlier discussions, the nature of the school milieu and educational system were to be the major focus. Committee objectives were established to create an interagency approach which would result in increased sensitivity at the community level to reduce the isolation of children from their regular environment; that is, to reduce segregation and encourage integration.

The Committee solicited reactions to a series of position papers (prepared by James Tompkins and Wilbur Lewis, an educator and child psychologist) which conceptualized a child advocacy system using the neighborhood school as a focal point. The concept of *ecological planning* and its implications for educational programs for emotionally disturbed children were outlined. In summary, the approach called for the creation of a school-based advocacy system providing for effective immediate intervention in difficult child environment transactions and for developing a design for new arrangements that fit children and their environments. This school-based approach was to involve:

- the public school(s);
- the families of children served by the school(s); and,
- the community agencies that intervened into or influenced child environments. Actually this was the initiation of what is now called "wrap-around" services for meeting the needs of children who are emotionally/ behaviorally disordered.

As a direct result of the solicited reactions to the position papers, the next move by the Committee was to recommended joint support for several model child advocacy proposals. From March until August 1970, the Committee developed a letter inviting proposal applications. During this period it shifted its emphasis from an essentially school-based approach to a community or neighborhood advocacy system.

In late 1970, BEH and NIMH decided to stimulate the development of a few school and neighborhood child advocacy demonstration programs, which were to strengthen the neighborhood's resources and capabilities for facilitating optimal development of children. The foremost goals were to:

- improve community resources and the delivery of services necessary for the emotional, social, and educational development of all children in a neighborhood; and,
- improve the environmental systems for children presenting behavioral or developmental problems.

In general, BEH and NIMH wanted to develop child advocacy programs that would:

- ensure that all children in a designated area have access to human services available in the community;
- identify needed (but unavailable) preventative and direct service and mobilize resources to initiate them; and,
- evaluate and improve the effectiveness of children's service both by formal research and by participation of parents and interested community members in decision-making affecting the initiation of programs or modification of old ones (Kahn, Kamerman, & McGowan, 1972, pp. 41–42).

The BEH-NIMH Joint Committee saw the creation of a child advocacy board as an essential component in the development of the child advocacy movement. This board, whose membership would represent children's interests, would have policy making responsibilities in conjunction with representatives of the community, including parents and residents as well as professionals.

While the BEH-NIMH committee was meeting, another committee was being formed including several heads from HEW and/or their representatives with the intent to discuss the implementation of the recommendations contained in the report of the JCMHC. On October 6, 1970, the committee met to discuss the importance of the Commission's recommendation that comprehensive child advocacy programs be established to involve all levels of government and private enterprise.

This group was to examine whether advocacy programs had the potential for:

- improving children's services;
- making communities more responsive and responsible;
- narrowing the gap between the scope and quality of services available and those required; and,
- increasing agency accountability.

Group members felt that advocacy did have great potential since it represented a way of securing sophisticated evaluation of current practices, meeting the needs of parents and the public for objective information, promoting cooperation among service programs, and encouraging community responsibility and agency accountability.

According to those attending, child advocacy was adequately defined within the JCMHC Report. The advocacy proposal was the mandate for a reordering of national priorities and involved:

- adequacy of services and service delivery;
- community responsiveness, responsibility, and accountability to and for children; and,
- involvement of both public and private sectors.

First, there was the need for planning and programs. The nature of children's needs was to be identified and necessary and appropriate resources determined. On-going children's programs might be utilized, but there was a need for better planning and cooperation. Second, there was the need for new ideas, improvement of existing practices, and more responsive methods of intervention. Third, there was the need for continuing evaluation of children's services, which called for studying the effectiveness of programs and services and assessing the resources of the community—the way they worked together and the degree to which they utilized the best available practices and knowledge. Fourth, there was a need to assure the legal rights of children, including the right to be treated properly physically and psychologically.

Chapter Three

National Institute of Mental Health's Highest Priority

Soon after his appointment as Director of the National Institute of Mental Health (NIMH) in June of 1970, Dr. Bert Brown indicated that the Institute's highest priority would be mental health programs for children. One of his first actions was to create the NIMH Committee on Child Mental Health in September of 1970. This newly created committee was to review the Institute's programs for children to recommend and, if needed, expand services. The Committee included a subcommittee on child advocacy, which subsequently formed the basis for the NIMH position to encourage inter-institutional cooperation in developing and providing services to children and their families through child and family advocacy programs.

The subcommittee on child advocacy recommended the study and implementation of methods for developing and exercising advocacy functions in existing programs such as community mental health centers, school systems, and other human service agencies as well as in programs/agencies independent of the human service system. It was recommended that training programs be initiated to prepare personnel to assume child advocacy roles and that these training programs be developed at all levels of government and in mental health centers and academic institutions. It also recommended that teaching materials and curricula for child advocacy training be developed.

The subcommittee members pointed out that children and young people have few means available to them to exert leverage upon those institutions that have an impact on their growth and development. While most other American population groups have at least the potential of creating advocates for themselves, children do not. Members of the subcommittee also stated that there was evidence that the well being of the child is highly related to the well being of the family, an observation that implied a need for including the family in an advocacy program.

The *family-child advocacy* program approach was defined as a consumer-controlled outreach system with two major objectives:

- To obtain more responsive, adequate, and effective service from child and family service agencies.
- To develop the strengths, skills, and initiative of families and communities to solve their own problems.

This approach was to include an analysis of the needs of children, families, and the community, and the development of a system of human services. The programs would foster family-centered preventive mental health concepts. The family-oriented program would be developed and directed by the citizen council. The director, an employed qualified professional in human services, would employ a staff of family and child consultants to work directly with families. The director and staff would serve as advocates for the families and children in the relationships they established with service agencies and collaborate with these agencies to improve delivery of required services to the child/family.

The second recommended approach was the *community advocacy* system. In this approach the professional or nonprofessional personnel identified as "child mental health advocates" would serve in child-serving agencies (i.e., health, mental health, education, recreation, criminal justice) as the agencies' "conscience" in relation to children's needs. The advocates would attempt to change policy, procedures, and practices within the agencies and improve coordination among them. They would obtain sanctions with the support or the community mental health center, mayor's office, and/or the health and welfare council.

Finally, the NIMH subcommittee recommended that child advocacy programs be instituted at state or regional levels. This approach was analogous to the approach suggested for communities. The thrust for advocacy at the state level might come from the governor's office through the state mental health authority, with the intent of changing policy, procedures, and practices of various child-serving agencies within a state to better serve children.

Chapter Four

Further Support for Child Advocacy: White House Conference on Children

On July 1, 1971, Jean Reynolds, Director, Office of Child Development (HEW), summarized suggestions about child advocacy from the proceedings of the White House Conference on Children. Reynolds indicated that seven of the 25 forums offered recommendations concerning the creation of an advocacy agency for children. Other recommendations were made about federal organizations for children and neighborhood centers.

The White House Conference recommendations suggested a variety of ways of furthering child advocacy—from continuing the Children's Bureau's involvement to establishing a federal department of children and youth, which would include a national advisory council on child advocacy. The proposed federal agency would have the responsibility of directing a national program of child advocacy involving state and local agencies, and organizations.

Two major themes were apparent in the Conference recommendations: (1) that the needs of every child be assessed and met and adverse conditions affecting children be removed, and (2) that the "voice of children" be heard in the highest levels of government.

The main objectives of an advocacy agency at any level of government would be to:

- ensure that all children's needs are known and met;
- create a united attack on areas of special concern;
- work for legislative, judicial, and administrative change that would bring about permanent rather than temporary improvement of children's circumstances;
- contribute to the improvement of existing services and to the development of new resources; and,
- bring about better coordination of services. (White House Conference, 1971, pp. 91, 92, 99).

It soon became apparent during the conference that to achieve these objectives, a national child advocacy office would have to serve as a catalyst and coordinate efforts to represent children's interests in the determination of policies and programs, and the allocation of resources. It would also be the responsibility of this office to develop national priorities and policies that pertain to children and to advise on children's needs and rights. A key to the success of the mandates of the office would be the encouragement of youth and adult consumers to participate in the development of programs and the delivery system to be utilized (White House Conference, 1971).

The White House Conference suggested that the director of the advocacy office be either a Cabinet member, or a person directly responsible to a Cabinet member, or a chairperson of a presidential council or commission responsible to a Cabinet member. The advocate office would receive both federal and private funding. Those involved should represent ethnic, cultural, and racial groups and should include parents and youth. The advocacy office should be a coordinating agency housing an interdepartmental committee to address all issues related to children in the Executive branch of government. Similarly, state advocacy offices should be developed and associated with the governor's office (White House Conference, 1971).

The White House Conference also recommended the development of local neighborhood and community advocacy boards. The membership of the boards, decided by the citizens, would determine children's needs and recommend services. The major role of the boards would be to marshal public opinion, to be cooperative, and to influence development and implement changes for children in need (White House Conference, 1971).

Another Conference recommendation concerned individual advocates who would provide information and refer those in need to resources. Such persons would provide a supportive relationship to enable persons to use resources and intercede on behalf of the child when necessary. The advocate would represent their interests or see that they were represented. The advocates would be based in a neighborhood or community. While this organization would work on behalf of individual children, they would also be their spokespersons and express the needs of the group. Both the advocates and the board would work for needed community and institutional change and for the creation of essential resources (White House Conference, 1971).

In the described organization the advocate is seen as a champion of children and a generalist, who attempts to achieve maximum use of existing community resources and seeks to avoid duplication of effort. The agency sponsoring the advocates should provide backup specialists such as lawyers and physicians. The advocate would work in concert with parents when possible, but would never usurp the parent's rights or responsibilities.

The national concern for the development of child advocacy programs was made clear during the 1970s and the forum for child advocacy activity became the U.S. Department of Health, Education and Welfare. The issues identified in this historical overview represent the concern, interest, and activities that were addressed in the late 1970s, however, not much has changed to the current day. There has been spotted activity on the part of the advocate in several sections of the country, but the overall situation has not moved forward to any great extent. The impediments to the movement shall be discussed in the following chapters but more action is certainly needed to spur the further development of child advocacy. Hopefully, the past efforts augur more activity in the 1990s on behalf of children and advocacy programs for children. It appears with the passage of state and federal legislation that the timing is now for the advocacy movement to become full cycle and bring forth some of the needed activity which to this point has only been debated.

Chapter Five

Advocacy Models: Child Advocacy in North Carolina

Child advocacy and the need to develop a child advocate movement was certainly not a new and unique idea to the professionals working in the State of North Carolina. Several professional groups and some laymen had been working on formulating the concept of child advocacy as an umbrella under which providing better services for children could be examined and problems resolved. These problems included fragmented services, inefficient delivery systems, and the continued institutionalization of children. Included in this list of problems was also the lack of knowledge concerning programs and programming for children, ineffective dissemination of current knowledge already in fold and our inability to positively influence in a more constructive way the lives of children. This was especially true for the children living in their natural social setting where many of the problems arise.

From the 1970s to the 1990s, the State of North Carolina and many of its local communities have established planning conferences, committees, and working groups to study the needs of emergent child advocacy procedures. An example would be the North Carolina Department of Mental Health supporting the following activities:

- Propositions to learn more about children in their own natural micro-cultural settings.

- Refinement of theoretical conceptions of the problem of disturbances in children.

- The need to provide more effective interventions relative to learning about children.

- The need to provide advocates for individuals when their personal development and integrity is jeopardized by the social systems in which they interact.

- The need to provide a mechanism in which the consumer can share responsibility for evaluation and making decisions about those services provided for him.

In accomplishing and implementing the above, activity proponents of the development of child advocacy in the State of North Carolina were aimed at:

- synthesizing the thinking and experience with child advocacy in North Carolina to date especially with regard to troubled and gifted children;

- obtaining a commitment to, and an investment in, the project from those agencies and individuals involved in child advocacy;

- conceptualizing the project as a way to learn more about advocacy through participation in a neighborhood laboratory rather than simply adding a program or service to a neighborhood; and,

- avoiding an expensive program that would reduce the feasibility of dissemination to other communities.

As a direct result of the above planning and activity in 1971, the North Carolina General Assembly created a Governor's Advocacy Commission on Children and Youth (Commission) to be located in the Department of Administration. The Commission was composed of seventeen members consisting of four youth members (below age twenty-one), four members of the North Carolina General Assembly, a representative of the

Superintendent of the North Carolina Department of Public Instruction, a representative of the Secretary of the Department of Corrections, and seven at-large members. The major powers and duties of the Commission included the following:

- To act as an advocate for children and youth within state local government and private agencies serving children and youth.
- To provide assistance in the development and coordination of child advocacy systems at all levels.
- To conduct reviews of existing programs for children and youth, evaluations of the delivery of services, and to review new programs prior to their implementation.
- To recommend new programs.
- To make recommendations to the governor and the general assembly concerning children's programs.
- To initiate studies relevant to the needs of children and youth.

The name of the Commission was changed to the Governor's Advocacy Council on Children and Youth and placed the Advocacy Council in the Department of Human Resources. The enactment of Chapter 1293 of the 1973 Session Law established the responsibility and the authority for the Council to make reports directly to the general assembly for the purpose of providing reports to the North Carolina Governor. Former Governors Robert Scott and James Holshouser appointed James R. Tompkins as the first Executive Director of the North Carolina Governor's Advocacy Council on Children and Youth.

Each state agency having responsibilities for providing services to children and their families were to be required to submit, at the request of the Council, a plan of services for children. The duty of acting as an advocate was expanded to include assisting children and their parents or guardians in obtaining services provided by state, local, and private agencies or organizations. Finally, the Advocacy Council had authority to hear appeals resulting from the denial of services to children by agencies under the jurisdiction of the Department of Human Resources.

In November of 1974, the Governor of North Carolina approved the formation of the North Carolina Office for Children within the Department of Human Resources. The Office for Children was created to provide coordination of effort in the planning for and delivery of services to children. Four primary areas of concern of the Office for Children were:

- Assistance to all children and their families in obtaining the services which are available and to which they are entitled.

- Services complementary to public school programs with emphasis on support systems for children with special needs and their families.

- Services for all preschool children who want and need services, including health services and quality child care.

- Assistance to consumer, religious, civic, and professional organizations, at both the state and local level, in promoting and developing interest and action on behalf of children and youth.

Additionally, the Office for Children was mandated to provide staff and support services to the Governor's Advocacy Council on Children and Youth. This mandate is the specific responsibility of the Advocacy Section of the Office for Children (Paul, Stedman, & Neufeld, 1977).

During 1974, the North Carolina Governor's Advocacy Council on Children and Youth was established as an independent private, non-profit organization. The underpinning rationale for this reorganization was that the very state agencies and bureaucracy it sought to change on behalf of children's program improvement impeded an internal governmental advocacy system. In spite of the professional staff of child-serving state agencies' awareness of and resistance to their bureaucratic shortcomings, outside advocacy was viewed as encroachment. Furthermore, it was assumed that the advocacy program should be free to intervene without internal sabotaging of the advocacy efforts and free to go to the governmental sources of power for cooperation and negotiation to resolve child advocacy issues.

Chapter Six

Child Advocacy in the 90s: A Definition

There are many different manifestations of child advocacy and many different frameworks within which it can be viewed. Among other things, child advocacy is an emerging social movement with increasing significance for the public, professional, and political communities. Unfortunately the concept has been emerging since the early 70s and has never fully blossomed to its full potential. However, child advocacy is becoming an important aspect of the general registration of concern for the welfare and human rights of children at the close of this twentieth century. This can be observed in three arenas - legislative, judicial and environmental. In the legislative arena, better laws to serve the constitutional rights of children such as the Individuals with Disabilities Education Act (IDEA) and the Americans with Disabilities Act (ADA) are being passed. As a result, the judicial arena is entering the picture with the adjudication of the regulatory aspects of the new legislation. Overall, the environmental aspect of the human social environments of children is on an upswing.

To date, child advocacy has been primarily committed to the ethic of freedom and expressed as a right of a child to be free to grow and have access to the resources necessary for that growth, including protection from impedance. Child advocacy has also provided a forum for articulating the ethic of individualism which has been expressed principally as the commitment to finding ways to ensure that the ownership of life choice rests with the child and the family and not with the service delivery system of bureaucracy. Both the ethic of freedom and the ethic of individualism have had great difficulty finding expression in existing social arrangements. The issue of a child as a responsible citizen has not been ethically or conceptually resolved. This resolution is complicated by the social and psychological dependency of children in American society.

Individualism and the right of a family to determine its own destiny have not been reconciled ethically or legally with the fact that some parents are psychologically and physically abusive to their children. Here in basic conflict are the child's freedom to grow and the parents' freedom to make decisions about their children, including those that are fundamentally destructive. The family's right to privacy makes it extremely difficult to learn about the realities that surround the child. (This lack of continuous ecological data poses problems for contemporary theories of child development and deviance as well as for advocacy.)

At the close of the twentieth century the child advocacy movement is evolving at many different levels and in many different environments. Still, it is extremely interesting and reassuring that much of the discussion about and commitment to advocacy as a movement for children is occurring within the bureaucracy as a kind of implicit commitment to renewal and relevance. The multifaceted and multiform nature of advocacy at this point, however, makes a systematic analysis of the issues very difficult, a situation which has encouraged considerable ambiguity in the development of advocacy programs to confront the issues.

While premature analysis or closure would most likely stifle much of the existing creative energy flowing into the child advocacy movement, there does need to be a quasi-systematic attempt to rather carefully articulate the conceptual substructures of advocacy. While child advocacy is not the domain of science, neither should it be immune to the well-developed tools of science. In some respects, child advocacy might provide some conceptual leverage for the renewal of the territory of science itself.

At present, there are numerous definitions of advocacy, each of which have certain values and some utility in the particular system in which it is used. Most of the existing definitions take their meaning from the contexts in which they are used. This relativity is part of the difficulty one runs into when trying to respond to the question, "What do you mean by child advocacy?" The existing definitions need to be examined carefully and the relationships between them assessed. The analysis of the conceptual meaning, the use of the term, and the perceived function of advocacy in different systems would provide some basic information about the movement itself and some insight, for example, into the basic issue of service vs. advocacy.

Another basic area of analysis involves the assumptions made in the definitions. What are the assumptions made about child growth and development, about deviance, about needs, about children? There is currently some work being conducted in the area of the conceptual basis for viewing child variance. The analysis of the assumptions about children made in the definitions of advocacy would assist in the larger enterprise of theory development as well as with the goals expressed in the advocacy movement. Those statements would vary within and among legislative, judicial, environmental, and economic concerns. Obviously, a better understanding of the goals of advocacy—as those goals are expressed by and in different systems—would provide basic information about the structure and direction of the movement itself. The analysis of the goal statements, assumptions, and definitions would represent the preliminary steps of generating some tentative working hypotheses about advocacy and dealing with the basic research questions. Although at this point it would be possible to shift from a use of the tools of philosophical analysis to the use of some of the empirical tools of science.

It is also important to analyze the procedures now associated with child advocacy. Child advocacy activities are proliferating at a rather rapid pace, and analysis in this area will be a significant undertaking. The evolution of advocacy, however, as a set of procedures (entry into a system, survival in a system, confrontation, adversary, etc.) must be brought into some kind of systematic understanding so that the procedures can be analyzed and improved over time. Procedural issues obviously are related to the particular area (legislative, judicial, environmental, and economic) in which they are articulated and practiced.

Such an investigation is a major and essential task at this point in time if there is to be some common understanding of and order to the advocacy movement. It is from this perspective that we can gain access to existing models of advocacy and, more importantly, develop the data that will assist in generating new models of advocacy. Data would provide a better understanding of what evaluation means as it relates to advocacy and assist with the basic issues that are now beginning to emerge (e.g., the behavioristic values of most evaluation methodologies vs. the rights of children). How do we deal philosophically and programmatically with the conflict (if there is one) between the values of behaviorism and those of humanism? The current values may be betrayed in the absence of personnel whose job is to humanize the environments of children. We have an overabundance of "specialists" in manipulating children.

A decision to embrace child advocacy has three important overall implications:

- Community responsiveness
- Responsibility
- Accountability

It means that the major evaluative criterion in the area of service delivery for children is adequacy, in contrast to the present pervasive and characteristic insufficiency. This means improvement in all respects for all children, not just the favored or the disadvantaged. The criterion of adequacy permits neither temporizing nor compromise. As advocacy calls for community responsiveness, responsibility, and accountability, neither the child nor the youth is able to know whether he or she is receiving adequate services or living in an optimizing environment, subsequently few parents can make these judgments. Even fewer of them are able to deal with the bureaucracy in a way to produce adequate services for their children even if they can define them. It is the community's responsibility to be responsive to the total needs of children, to work toward meeting these needs through both public and private efforts, and to hold those with obligations accountable in terms of excellence and adequacy (Hobbs, 1975).

It is clear that the achievement of adequacy and responsiveness must involve both public and private resources. It must involve federal, state, and municipal governments. One of the major problems is determining the division of labor. It is obvious to many that the needs of children are not being met. It is also clear that the infusion of more money and effort into delivery systems is not sufficient in itself to improve existing circumstances. There must be developed another element so that "good money doesn't follow bad money." Someone must be responsible for the continuing assessment of children's needs, for evaluating the adequacy of the community's performance, and for setting goals and schedules. This someone (or group of people) should not deliver services; however, he or she (or they) should be concerned with the delivery of services and be knowledgeable about them. In other words, time and attention must be given to advocacy for children-from spotting inadequacy to proposing how the jigsaw puzzle of services can be put together to produce results (Hobbs, 1975).

It is not enough to have a variety of services, parallel operations, and a molecular approach. Adequacy means uniformity, not islands of excellence and pockets of neglect and irresponsibility. Thus, advocacy must be exercised at all levels of government; it is one of the tasks of the advocate to work out and arrange the division of labor horizontally at each jurisdictional level and vertically among the various echelons. The private sector must be similarly covered. Advocacy becomes, therefore, a way of getting the job done, of measuring progress, of determining new needs and new approaches. Dependence upon fortuitous arrangements can no longer be tolerated (Hobbs, 1975).

Chapter Seven

Guiding Principles of Advocacy: Ecological Theory

In any advocacy movement there are several important principles that will serve as a guide for the movement. The major guiding principle is that every segment of the community should be actively involved from the start in the advocacy effort because each segment has certain resources that only it could contribute. In addition, active involvement of all segments reduces hostility between and among different segments and prevents ownership of the advocacy effort by any single segment.

The second guiding principle is that each segment of the advocacy movement should organize itself into a discrete unit. Within this discrete unit the membership can meet with one another to discuss common problems and concerns, find solutions, and, when necessary, present a united front. Their efforts can be coordinated to reduce duplication, overlap, waste, and competition, and increase the effectiveness of their service efforts. This group can also assist other segments of the community in their service efforts. Most importantly the unit could and should monitor the program efforts of the other segments of the community and intervene, if necessary, through formally established communication channels (Hines, 1987).

The last but rather important guiding principle is that representatives of each segment of the community must meet regularly to identify and investigate all areas of concern regarding the well being of the constituency in the community. The representatives must stride to work together to solve the problems and meet the needs of their constituents. During this meeting period there will be time to share expertise and resources while coordinating all service efforts in the community. These mandatory meetings will increase communication, trust, and cooperation among the different segments of the community. Thus, with mutual trust and understanding they will act together as a strong, united force to advocate the needs of the constituency at a statewide level (Hines, 1987).

The guiding principles are the underpinnings to create a conceptual and practical system of advocacy for children that will help children to acquire, retain, restore, and use appropriate, specific adaptive skills and maximize their potential as children. This will include the development of improved procedures for identifying the needs of children, the utilization of a consumer-oriented service delivery system, the training of child advocates, and the implementation of programs in public settings. It is our belief that these activities are of the highest priority, and that they represent an approach that will eventually result in a complete reconfiguration of existing programs and services for children—a reconfiguration that is long overdue.

Ecological theory is a theory of interaction that examines the dynamics of social exchange. Behavior is a major player in the basis of this theory. Deviance (a behavior per se) is not reducible to an individual difference but is rather a register of discomfort or disorder in a social system (Paul, Neufeld, Pelosi, 1977).

There is a positive correlation between the complex social and economic patterns that emerge with population growth and the complexity of socializing children. The world is complex and dynamic, and it is changing along with the social expectations for satisfactory adjustment and with respect to the behavior required for survival. We have not kept pace in social changes concerning the provisions we make for children to learn about themselves and the world. The roles of the institutions have changed, including the role of the family in raising children. The reduction of time parents have with children, the disappearing extended family, the rise of school failure, child abuse, and drug usage have all made a significant impact on the changing social and economic patterns of today. The vacuum created by the loss of family strength in influencing the character development of children has not been explicitly filled by another institution (Paul, 1971; Moynihan, 1993).

A "fit" between the requirements of the child's needs and his/her environments provides the child with opportunity for maximum growth. When there is a "misfit" between the child and external arrangements, there is trouble for both the child and his/her environment in the agitated exchange that evolves. This trouble is often resolved by the eventual extrusion of the child from the environment to create a calm in the transactions in that environment (Rhodes, 1967; Lewis, 1970).

Our failure to design arrangements which maximize the potential of children and our extrusion by default of many children from the arrangements (family, school, etc.) on which they are most dependent for their required "fits" are the basic problems faced by those responsible for what is happening to children. Childhood deviancies such as emotional disturbance or giftedness are labels that result from misfits between child and arrangements. These and several other "misfits" have created great suffering and frustration for children, parents, teachers, and other community members and will continue to do so until the proper intervention is in place (Paul, 1971; Moynihan, 1993).

We have most often acted as if the "trouble" is the exclusive property of the child. Occasionally, we have located the problem exclusively in the child's environment. These philosophical points of view and institutional responses are paralleled by advocacy groups which press for response to needs of particular children or to particular needs of children (Rhodes, 1967; Paul, 1977).

Rarely has attention been given to the social process-what happens between child and environment-which results in trouble and eventually in extrusion. We believe that there is a need for points of view, designed responses to problems, and advocacy which are concerned with "fits" between children and arrangements and the process by which the "fit" is either arranged or aborted. *The ecological point of view is concerned with man's adapting. It is concerned with the relationship between persons and environments. It searches for solutions that are addressed to the constant, ongoing, intricate interplay between man and environment(s). It locates human problems at points of "misfits" in the flow between two separate units (man and environment) of one single system. It treats the individual and his setting at context as a single complex system* (Rhodes, 1967; Lewis, 1970).

One way of thinking about how the process of extension is set in motion by the "misfit" is the notion of a "scanner." An individual or a behavior is "deviant" and thus a candidate for being moved out of "normal" settings only when he/she has been observed and so labeled. In this identification process, a scanner looks at behavior and asks first if it is expected and then if it is acceptable. If it is either unexpected, unacceptable, or both, a given behavior is likely to be defined as deviant. In making decisions about expectability and acceptability of behavior and response to it, the scanner uses not only the information gained in direct observation but also data concerning the environment in which the act was performed, the responses of other scanners, etc. Once a behavior has been defined and responded to as deviant, the actor is faced with the decision of repeating or not repeating the act. If the behavior recurs, the actor is most often labeled as "not fitting" and thus moved out of the setting in which the behavior is unexpected, unacceptable, or both. This, the extrusion which is so often the response to identified deviance, can be viewed not as something which exists inside an individual actor but as the result of a process of scanning, identification, and response to behavior which involves both actor and observer (Rhodes, 1970; McLauglin, 1995; Lewis, 1970).

The position adopted here, therefore, is that it is neither adequate nor accurate to define our tasks in terms of either problems with or of children or with or of the environments of children. Instead, our task must be defined in terms of the problems that occur in the exchanges or transactions between children and their environments. Such definition places some strain on our accustomed ways of thinking about and responding to the needs of children. To locate the difficulty in the transactions is to require alternative ways of thinking about and managing child-environment transactions and intervening in those transactions that are faulty or abortive.

Chapter Eight

Advocacy Needs of Children

This nation has always been measured by its tolerance, courtesy and generosity. America contributes and supports worldwide worthy causes except its affection and benevolence for its own children. A national incoherence prevails about compassionate intervention for children. There appears indifference about the welfare of children. One political party disparages advocates for children as bleeding heart liberals. The other political party concedes on children's requirements but reneges on funding. America is unwittingly coagency in our children's demise, abuse and neglect. The United States has historically contributed to warlike, hostile and tyrannical worldwide governments and is riddled with scandal, larceny, bribery, waste and pork-barreling. All the while our children fill jails, detention centers, institutions, kill themselves, kill others, seek refuge in savage gangs and are sexually and physically abused and/or neglected. Abuse victims lose love, trust, self-esteem, happiness, innocence, their childhood and their families. Child abuse is also linked to crime, homelessness, alcoholism, drug abuse, prostitution, suicide, teenage runaways and a variety of physical and mental disorders.

Part of the problem, then, is our failure as a society to effectively mediate necessary resources to children through our primary institutions (family and school). It seems reasonable to wonder how much our large and awkward social and physical structures established to serve children have become part of the problem for children. For example, part of the behavior maintenance structure of the observer or monitor (in groups or society at large) is its system of response to deviance. One major aspect of that system which will be described here is that of stigma. If an ecologically significant discrepancy occurs, behavior does not proceed as usual. The group, the observer, or the monitor registers the intolerable difference and searches for an ecologically relevant explanation. For example, a child in school is expected to "behave" and learn. Aberrance in school, then, is typically related to the child's behavior and learning incompetence or exceptionality. The focus of explanation is on the source of the "noise." The monitor does not examine its own process of monitoring. Neither does it examine the relationship between what it monitors and itself. The cultural violator not the cultural breach is the object of explanation (Paul, 1977; Pelosi, 1971; Moynihan, 1993).

Once the explanation for the behavior is determined, a label can be assigned to the child whose behavior caused the unrest. For example, the child who is significantly slow in school may be viewed as dumb and eventually labeled mentally retarded. Another child, highly talented or gifted, may be viewed as arrogant and disrespectful, then seen as disturbed. The label then leads to doing something with the child designed to restore calm and conformity in the group. This frequently involves extruding the child from the setting.

Labeling and stigma is the social means by which groups protect themselves in specific settings. It is a process of cultural quarantine where the rich are protected from the poor; the controlled are protected from the uncontrolled; the sane from the crazy; the normal from those with disabilities.

In summary:

- The person who has ecologically relevant different behavior is stigmatized for his difference.

- Decisions made about him/her are primarily based on group maintenance in contrast to child development criteria.
- The child has no advocate to represent his/her interests and is therefore vulnerable.
- Stigmatizing involves moral and ethical issues.

To aggravate the problem, this process registers the focus of responsibility for "the problem" and the focus of intervention in the child. We develop special services and arrangements for the *child's problem* or the *problem child* independent of outside influences or, if you will, the *system* as the *problem*.

Today, the public school may be the most serious cultural anachronism...our sense of community is dead. The intact cultural microcosms in which the idea of neighbor is as critical to the viability of the microcosm as is the institution of school may no longer exist. The cultural phenomenon of school is the significant community ally in preparing children for life, and the micro-culture now is in serious question. It is not surprising that the experience of diversity and disunity should result in alienation, and that the general experience of alienation should give rise to a revival of community and their schools. The trigger for this revival has been the lack of effective alliances among the child socializing agents either in the strategy and rules of child rearing or a shared commitment to the desired outcome of such a process (Paul & Pelosi, 1971; Sarason, 1990).

The attempt is to reformulate the mission of the school and from that point to make some sense out of its methods. The recent responses to this particular crisis have been to "advocate for heterogeneity" in the school, or at a minimum to "advocate for the interests of the individual child in the system." Advocacy for the child, which draws a line between his/her interests and the self-sustaining interest of the institution, has so far been formulated more in terms of educational process. In the context of the school, the typical classroom, then, is a time-limited, age-grade specific setting that brings together but does not necessarily unify several cultures and variable experiences within any one culture. There are rights of entry, of place, and of passage. The teacher is a decision maker who acts as the gate keeper of those rights, those rights being at any point in time and space an interaction of the various sets of rules, experiences, and aspiration. The only unity imposed on the structure is that of the institution of school itself. Children with disabilities may test or strain this system with their already formulated characterologies, learning, or behavioral differences (Paul & Pelosi, 1971; Smith, 1997).

The ecology of the classroom may be said to exist in a state of more or less equilibrium depending on the *"fit"* between all aspects of that ecology. That is, transactions proceed in a way that maintains or develops the setting and satisfies the transactors. *Fit* is a concept of positive experience in a space-time.

These are several *"fits"* that would be considered in the classroom:

- The peer fit between the child and other children.
- The child-curriculum fit between the child and the program, content, methods, and objectives for him/her.
- The child-teacher fit.
- The children-teacher fit.
- The fit between the child and the physical setting.
- Between the group and the physical setting.
- Between the teacher and the physical setting, etc.

The matrix on page 47 indicates the various combinations.

When a misfit occurs, that is a negative space-time experience, it may be ignored, negotiated, or dealt with by a unilateral decision based on the power structure of the arrangement.

It should be pointed out that the matrix categories differ significantly in the degree of openness for change and the power invested for significant decisions. For example, in a misfit between a gifted child and the school, change is almost always expected in the child rather than the school. When a misfit occurs between a troubled child and the teacher, it is the teacher who has the authority to make decisions relative to the misfit. The directionality of the change, then, can be understood in part as a result of this particular arrangement—institutions and schools remain rather static (Paul, 1977; Pelosi, 1971).

The public school is a repository of cultural diversity. The press to reduce that diversity in the public school has been successful primarily because of the ecological management tactics of schools. That is, the children are kept over time in the school setting physically arranged and scheduled relative to the primary message array of the school. After awhile in a traditional classroom, for example, all 30 children face the front of the room, sit up straight in their seats, listen to the teacher - that is, they look and act and talk like students. When they do not act like students, there are consequences to force them into that role, the only acceptable role for a child to "fit" that school (Paul, 1977; Sarason, 1990).

The problem, then, is to provide the child with some continuity of experience, protection from being made scapegoat by

	Child	Children	Teacher	Physical Setting	School	Curriculum
Child	X					
Children		X				
Teacher			X			
Physical Setting				X		
School					X	
Curriculum						X

cultural, social, and expectation wars between school, home, and neighborhood, and support in coping with cultural diversity and developing competencies in tasks for different settings for gifted and troubled children. It is further to provide support for teachers and parents to negotiate their differences and develop more adequate child supportive behaviors (Paul, 1977; Lewis, 1970).

The concept of "goodness of fit" clearly includes the family and the community for services to match the child's needs; community agencies and families in alliance with child and schools (Paul, Pelosi, and Ray, 1976).

Chapter Nine

Child Advocacy: Its Purpose

Child advocacy is the development of an activist child support structure closely related to the home, community, and school experiences of children. The neighborhood and the proposed structure should serve as a laboratory for learning more about:

- the child;
- the neighborhood-specific systems of socialization and the process by which children in that neighborhood become identified as special; and,
- the consequences of that identification and labeling as a basis for reformulating out interventions into the child's life.

The broad purposes of child advocacy are to:

- create a neighborhood system of advocacy for children that will support the children's acquisition, retention and use of age appropriate, phase specific adaptive skills and maximize their potential as children;
- support the development of ecological integrity to the mutual benefit of the child and his home, school, and neighborhood environment; and,
- develop a more adequate understanding of the child and his ecology and the operations necessary to support both, e.g., training, shared responsibility, and interventions.

Four generalized goals seem appropriate to child advocacy. These goals being:

- to increase or facilitate in neighborhood or community interventions which reduce the stigma and exclusion of children from their regular or required programs or environments;

- to secure maximal gains for the child if the child must be moved from one program or environment to another;

- to create programs or environments in which a "good fit" between children and program or environment is negotiated with increased participation of children and their parents; and,

- increased parent/child participation results in programs and/or environments that meet the needs of the individual child.

In addition to the four generalized goals listed above there are specific goals that are more operational in the development of a child advocacy movement. The specific goals and their rationale base are:

- *Monitor (scan) child and environmental (program) fits to maximize child potential and environment integrity.*

There currently exist a limited number of environments for children. Having placed so much responsibility on these environments (school and home primarily) for all children, the need to know the quality of transactions within them is paramount. To leave the development of children to chance by not knowing what occurs and by requiring minimal (in the schools) or no (in the home) competency in child engaging skills does not make child or cultural sense.

- *Increase community awareness of the need to increase environmental alternatives for children.*

In the discarding or absence of programs or environments that hold potential for "goodness of fits" for certain child needs, a community might consider creating programs or environments to intervene early in the learning and socialization process.

• *Create alternate child-relevant programs or environments.*

Regular classrooms in the public schools are primarily designed to give attention to cognitive aspects of child development. New environmental or program arrangements within schools, within individual classrooms, before and after school, or even in transportation arrangements between school and home could give attention to socialization. Aspects for the child and school curriculum might be designed to better meet the needs of children from different cultural groups who bring with them to school a variety of values, behaviors, and experience with different reward systems.

• *Create alliances among families, schools, and other community interests who have a primary interest in maximizing child programs and environments and thus child potential.*

It seems likely that the effectiveness of individual efforts will be increased if community, family, and school join together in an alliance designed to serve the needs of children rather than pursuing special interests, special needs, etc. in separate or even competitive arenas.

• *Catalyze the existing programs.*

Coordination and integration of existing programs for efficient delivery of services and avoiding "cracks" in the service system through which children fall.

• *Reduce stigma and program exclusion due to poverty and/or labeling.*

Help professionals and families via training, consultation, and advocacy to acquire a "goodness of fit" between the child and environment (program) in spite of prevailing social focus or obstacles.

- *Mobilize informed neighborhood and community advocacy resources for children.*

There exist many resources in communities for children that are usually not deployed. These include high school students, older people, married couples with no children, and organizations such as churches and youth organizations. These natural life structures of the community could serve as support for children in leading off alienation and providing advocacy for inclusion into a good fit in the environment or programs (Pelosi, 1971; Paul and Pelosi, 1971; Paul, 1977).

Chapter Ten

Child Advocacy: A Proactive View

Child advocacy is action oriented, not a passive strain, and it has been stated earlier that it is a social, political, and professional movement to improve and safeguard the best of children's life circumstances. Child advocacy characteristics, purposes, definitions, and underpinning values and belief systems have been examined and several references have been made about parental and professional engagement in advocacy program development. In addition there has been a critical analysis of current practices. However, there are specific conceptual issues that need to be discussed and outlined that will facilitate program design in the future.

The specific philosophy behind any child advocacy movement is to improve the total resources and delivery of services for the comprehensive development of all children. In general, child advocacy programs should ensure that children have access to whatever human services they need that are now available in the community, to identify needed preventive and direct services that are not available, and mobilize resources to initiate those services. A child advocacy program specifies the provision of adequate services for children, the development of community responsiveness to children's needs, and the provision of local resources and development of programs.

Children's services should be systematically evaluated. Not only does this mean studying the effectiveness of programs and services but also includes the capability to know the resources of the community, the way they work together, and the degree to which they utilize the best in current practices and knowledge about children's services.

Finally, there is the need to assure the legal rights of children. Children have a right to adequate living arrangements, food, clothing, education, medical attention, and the like. In light of these concerns, we should view and define advocacy as the process of constructing programs connecting children to appropriate child serving agencies. Agencies should assume this goal with mutual responsibility and cooperate on a planned, coordinated basis. The implementation of this concept would assure that all children with needs would receive maximum attention from available resources. When this has been accomplished, then the focus on child advocacy in a community would be the development of various community groups and agencies with clear commitments to children. This includes the mutual ascribing and accepting of precise roles to act in concert for the children in need. At the state level, child advocacy means that all agencies with priorities for children work together and operates as a coordinated delivery system building mutual responsibility and coordination at all levels. Interagency efforts are needed to increase the sensitivity to the "why" and "how" children are isolated from their normal and natural environments. These interagency efforts should agree to increase the assessment of programs that isolate children from their normal and natural environments, thereby reducing the isolation of children. At the same time the process of developing more successful plans in returning isolated children to their normal and natural environments will be an ongoing effort.

Not every person or agency in a community is going to embrace the development of a comprehensive child advocacy initiative. In fact, statements such as the ones listed below make up a partial list of many of the communities' initial reaction to a child advocacy movement.

Statements or rationale for non-activity include:

- Why advocacy? Things are going well for most children.

- There is no money available.
- There are no resources available.
- There is no expertise available.
- We are doing our best.
- What can you do for them anyway?
- They are hopeless and stupid.
- They are delinquent and handicapped.

Child and youth advocacy programs challenge these recurring responses to the needs of children. There are in fact several challenges that present themselves to the developing child advocacy movement.

Some of the challenges are:

- finding a solution to fit the child rather than to fit the child to the solution;
- to create engineering capacities to help our child serving agencies to reassess policies, standards, procedures and practices;
- to hold ourselves and them (others) accountable to sustain appropriate goals and programs on the basis of children's needs; and,
- to attract individuals and groups of parents, citizens, and professionals at all levels to pick up the gauntlet on behalf of children.

In order for the child advocacy movement to become proactive in its view, the process must seek to champion for the rights of all children and to make every child's needs known and met. The proactive child advocacy movement will be developed and centered around the following activities:

- An examination of the process of how children who deviate are labeled and categorized on a deviance model at the local or state level.

- Examine the process of how children who deviate are referred, isolated and excluded.

- Examine the process of how children who deviate are mismatched or misfit to treatment, rehabilitation, and educational programs.

- Maintain children who deviate with their families and in their communities.

- Maintain children who deviate in regular schools and community programs.

- Minimize institutionalization of deviant children.

- Minimize use of residential programming.

- Minimize use of individual psychotherapy.

- Minimize use of special education classes.

- Arrange with child serving agencies (including public schools) a coordinated planning and program effort that reduces overlapping services, referrals, isolation, and extrusion of deviant children.

- Arrange with child serving agencies commitments for assuming mutual responsibility and accountability for children they purport to serve.

- Arrange with child serving agencies procedures to return children to their normal and regular environments.

- Document and record how children are systematically discriminated against due to social, mental, and physical deviancy for the better understanding of agency/institutional response to children and to utilize this information and data on a within-system operation to modify agency/institutional policies and procedures for a more appropriate response to children's needs.

- Create parent-citizen community councils to assess program policies and procedures of child serving agencies for the purposes of introducing program modifications and accountability.

- Create legal-judicial advisory boards to consult with child advocacy personnel regarding the legal rights of children, and what legal options are available to assist agencies/institutions to more appropriately serve children, and for parents to advocate/demand such appropriate services.

The above may be used as a checklist to facilitate the development of the proactive movement and to systematize the steps that are necessary for the adoption of such a movement.

Child advocacy purports to react to all children's needs. However, experience directs child advocacy attention to the different or deviant child. The different or deviant child is one who is systematically excluded simply on the basis of deviancy. Children are segregated and fitted into life situations that perpetuate their "differences" or deviancy whose vulnerable characteristics range from slight to great in comparison with the larger child population and who find themselves so labeled.

In a sense, child advocacy has been and will continue to be characterized as representing the personal and practical needs and requirements of children where/when the children and their natural advocates cannot ably represent themselves in fulfillment of those personal and practical needs. Individuals, citizen groups, professional groups, and alliances of all these groups can assume advocacy roles for children's needs and requirements. When assuming this role the child advocacy becomes a social movement which assumes a set of beliefs regarding children and their rights to be loved, for security and protection to grow, learn, and be competent, happy individuals.

As a social movement the child advocacy plan is to systematically:

- investigate and gather data regarding societal responses, or lack of responses, to meet the children's needs;
- document that societal response;
- illustrate and dramatize societal values and responses to children;
- arbitrate and negotiate a renewal of societal values to create a more responsive societal reaction to children's needs; and,
- hold societal supported "groups" accountable for their responses to children via parent and legal advocacy groups.

When the child advocacy movement becomes a social movement and the above are systematically implemented, then the beliefs that the system should maintain about children comes into play. In the social movement child advocacy dimension, the beliefs about children are:

- Children have a right to information about how and why decisions are made about what happens to them at home, in schools and in communities.
- Children have a right to make decisions about themselves whenever possible.
- Children have a right to be free from discriminatory labels and specialized programs whenever possible.
- Children have a right to remain at home, in community and regular environments, whenever possible.

Child advocacy as seen in the social movement context also holds a set of beliefs about child serving agencies. These beliefs are as follows:

- Most child serving agencies are organized essentially to maintain themselves as institutions and are engaged in activities that perpetuate the maintenance of professional biases, territoriality, and practices that militate against the best interests of children.

- Most child serving agencies are organized to engage in activities that place the burden of child deviance within the child rather than regarding external factors that influence, determine, and reinforce child deviance.

- Most child serving agencies are organized to avoid the implementation of challenging programs for the more deviant child and accept the less deviant child, and unwittingly mismatch the less deviant child they accept with very often inappropriate and "failing" programs.

- Most child serving agencies are organized to diagnosis, label, refer, isolate, and exclude the more needy and deviant child.

- Most child serving agencies unwittingly perpetuate professional incompetence through the practice of being "long on talk" (conferences and memos) and short on developing and implementing practical and sound childhood programs.

- Most child serving agencies are prepared to intimidate natural and professional child advocates to maintain their status quo and tenuous reputations.

In addition to the above beliefs, there is also a set of beliefs concerning the personnel that serve children in the child advocacy movement. These beliefs include that the serving personnel:

- are threatened by deviance;

- are passive in the face of promoting challenging children's programs;

- are untrained or mismatched with certain children related to their own training and experience;

- assume a spectator role with children rather than a participant role with children;

- sometimes hate and physically and psychologically abuse children;
- sometimes support racist and other demeaning attitudes and practices;
- sometimes support dehumanizing programs under the guise of implementing professional programs such as the use of aversive stimulation or reinforcement a.k.a. behavior modification; and,
- finally, most child serving personnel are of good will and open for change but are not supported by the bureaucratic and systematic approaches of agencies to ensure the discontinuance of mediocre programs.

Child advocacy supports the concept that existing and new legislation and programs should be systematically coordinated within major state and federal agencies, assuming commitment for accepting mutual responsibility and accountability for children.

Child advocacy supports the position that Offices of Child Advocacy be initiated at federal, state, and local levels, and that the political and structural approaches to child advocacy should be oriented to the further development and implementation of child programs, for their coordination and for their accountability (Tompkins & Brooks, 1977).

Chapter Eleven

A Case Study: Individual Child Advocacy

Shane is a four-year-old black child who attends a small rural elementary public school in a Southern State. Shane was on the edge of program exclusion from this school's early education program for at-risk economically disadvantaged children. Shane lives with his single mother whose energies for control and limit setting on Shane has expired. He dominated his mother and simply did what he pleased...unchecked. He ate what he pleased and when he pleased. He left home for long unsupervised trips in the neighborhood. He screamed, hit and generally terrorized his mother.

The early education teachers in his school program described Shane as seriously troubled and sometimes dangerous. Shane was unaffected and unresponsive to the typical interventions to control his excessive physical and verbal aggression among other disturbed behaviors. So, in this context, what we tried to develop was an unpretentious collage of a benevolent, compassionate covenant with Shane. We didn't see Shane as a toad or turnip...but as a child at risk.

The therapeutic landscape of the school program needed a reorganization or reorientation of environmental influences for a troubled child where normal desires Shane regards as being important are satisfied or hope they will be satisfied. These important normal desires are being pleased with oneself, being friends with others, and obtaining basic emotional and physical needs. We aspired to influence the pattern of Shane's life at school and home which included the prospect of experiencing some kind of joy by some markedly favorable turn of circumstances. We tried to enhance his freedom from anxiety, restlessness, and discouragement as life experiences. The emotional furniture of the child's mind should be belief in himself and capability of becoming transcendent from difficulties, and where the child becomes more conscious of himself, behavior, and makes exertions and efforts to change. We tried to harmonize these forces into a landscape of promise.

The program provided well-conceptualized and implemented early education activities for approximately fifteen four-year-old boys and girls from this rural and economically plighted area of the South. The staff included a capable master's level educator certified in this area of education. Two effective, sensitive aides supported the program activities. The program was organized around a permissive orientation combining highly structured activities with large time segments of unstructured play, supervised and manipulated by the staff. The equipment, materials, toys, and other props were new, varied, and plentiful. The program provided group and child-by-child activities designed to meet the unique needs of each child. The educational plans were oriented toward meeting entry skill requirements of school and making life a little easier and more fun for child and parent. The curriculum emphasized developmental activities suitable for young children that focused on skill improvement and knowledge acquisition that are generalizable to other educational settings.

The major goal of the curriculum was to assist each child in reaching a greater degree of independence. The organization of the curriculum reflected a system of priorities and values that emphasize development of cognition and language based on developmental considerations. The curriculum attempts to:

- isolate the methods, materials, and contingencies under which each child functions effectively;

- decelerate previously specified behavioral excesses;
- accelerate behaviors appropriate for sound or functional behaviors; and,
- provide assistance for the child's entry into the next phase of education progress.

Shane was observed during several visits for approximately five hours. Shane was notably different compared with the other children in physical appearance, socialization, and general behavior. Shane was overweight at 150 pounds; and nearly continually at discordance with the adults, children and program. Some of Shane's behavioral reactions were:

- Continual aimless wandering and ambling around the schoolroom; complete disengagement from program activities.
- Pervasive distracting and apparent inability to organize his own play experience.
- Constant movement from area, from toy, from one subgroup to another.
- Frequent testing and violation of established limits, expectations and behavioral boundaries typically organized for an early education program.
- Intrusive interference with other children's play spiced with aggressive hitting, pushing, grabbing, knocking into, stepping on, and in the way of other's behaviors.
- Aggressive snatching of other children's toys and/or destruction of other children's projects.
- Attending or engagement behavior limited to approximately five minutes on an intermittent basis.
- Inability to attend or respond to typical directions, limits, or structuring procedures.
- Exhibited a spacey, "out of touch," far away demeanor.

- Easily over-stimulated and excitable at unexpected stimuli or some of the typical but noisy group activities.
- Appeared flat—blunted in reacting with genuine or appropriate affect especially anxiety or guilt in wrong doing.
- Did not seek out or reach out for adult support or relationship. (There appeared a detachment from children and adults regarding relationship building or enjoyment of relationships.).
- Did not respond to typical behavior control interventions;
- Exhibited a primitive, infantile reaction to food at meal time situations.
- Appeared to have little sensitivity to other's space.

In the review of several months of Shane's behavior, it was teacher documented that Shane exhibited frequent, day-to-day outbursts of aggression, swearing, and sexual profanity.

A training conference with the school principal, the master teacher and aides after school for approximately three hours was initiated. This activity included a detailed review of Shane's present behaviors, program intervention prescription, and follow-up activities that led to the following intervention.

The school had already assigned one teacher aide to Shane for one-to-one care and supervision. It was recommended that the aide meet Shane each morning the very moment he arrived at the classroom. It was decided that when Shane arrived, the aide should take Shane off to the side or corner of the room, away from the other children and distant from the toys or equipment. During this time the aide should discuss with Shane the expectations all the teachers have about his behavior, and his need to enjoy himself without having trouble or problems. This quiet time should extend for several minutes with Shane verbalizing with the aide's help the commitment to behave and obey the teachers. Shane must not leave the chair or have a toy during this quiet time. The aide may say the following:

> You may watch the other children play, but now and only for a few minutes you must stay with me. And how are you doing this morning? Do you feel good? Is everything OK at home? Do you think you will be able to do what I ask? Will you obey me?

After some conversation and interviewing and when the aide feels Shane is not troubled and tending toward misbehavior, the aide may then review the basic expectations and rules expected in preparation for entry into his tailor-made program.

This type of quiet time interaction was recommendation for implementation periodically throughout the day. If Shane were non-compliant during these times, Shane would not be allowed into program entry and must remain with the aide until both agree upon his commitment to comply and try to have fun without getting into trouble. Of foremost importance, the aide identified any opposition behavior and reflected by verbalizing for him how that kind of behavior caused him trouble.

During this time and throughout the day there was consistent firm, and succinctly stated behavior expectations. The adults verbalized and cautioned with succinct reminders about appropriate behavior. There were no long discussions. The messages for Shane were that expectations were to be responsive and conform. That was the way he could enjoy himself.

When Shane complied, the aide and other adults would be generous with praise, affection, compliments, and verbal support, explaining and reflecting how well he was doing, how wonderful he was and how much fun he was having. The adults needed to verbalize, explain, and reflect in precise language the appropriate behavior and how desirable that good behavior was.

After each periodic separation Shane had from the morning quiet time and the ones subsequent during the day, Shane would be introduced into a small group. Shane was not allowed to wander or amble around the room. Shane was not allowed to participate in full group activities. The small group activity with two or three other children were to be highly structured play activities that used only a few toys or props that supported the activity. This group activity would be in the more quiet and less traveled part of the room. The aide helped Shane participate and cautioned him, explained the activity and provided clarifications, and verbal assistance throughout the program.

During the activity the aide observed Shane constantly. During this time Shane would be praised and complimented on how well he was doing. If Shane became oppositional and ignored limit setting, Shane would be removed from the group and only re-integrated upon observable compliant behavior.

If the adults felt it was important for Shane to be part of a large group activity, Shane would remain on a one-to-one correspondence with the aide. Shane was not permitted to participate in large group dance or movement activities, that produced excitement, with the other children. He could sit on the aide's lap or help the adults prepare the props, equipment, and toys.

During periodic snack and meal times, Shane would remain with the aide and only one or two other children. The aide would help by instructing Shane about acceptable eating behavior. Shane was not allowed random movement during this time.

When the adults noted Shane's spacey "out of touch" behavior, they would firmly get him to attend to conversation and dialogue with them. Shane was encouraged and praised for responding and interacting with the adults during these times.

When Shane displayed planned deliberate limit testing, the aide quickly provided immediate interventions. This interference and management effort occurred at the very emergence of unacceptable behavior and at each occurrence of the unacceptable behavior.

The staff intervened with all hitting, pushing, knocking, bumping, stepping on behavior immediately and moved Shane away from the other children with explanations for the removal.

The staff interfered with Shane's intrusive behavior on other children's individual or group play. At these times Shane was helped to discover an individual play experience for himself and given assistance, support, and praise for his successful engagement.

The staff scanned the milieu and all its program components to determine what triggered his misbehavior. Upon identification of environmental seduction for misbehavior, the staff organized preventative measures to assist Shane in a productive activity.

When episodes such as aggression, verbal assaultiveness, or sexual and other swearing behaviors appeared, Shane was held and removed from the room as soon as possible. In agreement with the principal, and on these extreme incidents, the aide and principal had a joint interview with Shane about the misbehavior. Consequences for those misbehaviors were developed and applied after careful explanation to Shane.

The procedures described represented the essential proposed intervention at school for Shane. In summary they reflected these program management interventions:

- Provision of a highly structured program with a one-on-one coverage.

- Provision of extensive praise and reinforcement for acceptable behavior.

- Provision of a highly gratifying program experience within small groups.

- Frequent adult verbalization and reflections for Shane about what he is doing and how it will get him into trouble.

- Clearly stated expectations.
- Intense efforts helping Shane discover happiness in relationships and how he can reach out to others.
- Systematic periodic interviewing, structuring, explanations in preparation for each new experience.
- Scan environmental triggers that are seductive to Shane's misbehavior and remove or modify those influences.
- Continual adult display of affection, praise, support, and encouragement.

After a three-week, six-week, and nine-week follow up, teachers reported that Shane had benefited in a remarkable manner. There was a near total reduction in physical and verbal aggression. The staff reported Shane was more tranquil, engaged in program activities, less spacey, less aimless ambulatory behavior and more related to children and adults. The changes have been dramatic.

In this described situation there are adults and the environmental influences that are dedicated in a willing, practical, and thoroughgoing place for affection and devotion to help children transcend their adjustment difficulties. They all are bound in interpersonal ties with mutually related roles. Sometimes adults subordinate their private interests in favor of giving what is due to children and their best interests. This interaction is not one-sided. It is not that children are forced to engage in the academic or therapeutic programs, but rather that they do so because the activities of learning accord with their interests and needs.

There are children's resistance and personal adjustment difficulties; but there is an expectation they will initiate and sustain more acceptable behavior. Adults expect children to begin to want academic and social success. Though this disposition may be latent, it is expected to be nascent.

A major source of children's aggression is when they are frustrated in their attempt to satisfy their desire and want to be better learners and better socialized. Children know what they want in spite of defensive activities. It is expected, via the therapeutic setting, that they know to want to be better. Therein, these conscious forces are manipulated in the setting. The wanting to be better gives rise to actions to be better. However, something must happen in the environment and in children, which results in the antecedent influences to work for their betterment.

Children should be free, autonomous and responsible to some extent. That they seek adult approval and help in becoming less anxious are powerful motivators for self-consciousness, self-improvement, and self-evaluation.

Therapeutic practices should reflect, not negate, reasonable group, societal, and civilized rules, norms and values...but they are not uniquely contrived to ameliorate failure. Life is always a problem, an insecurity, a "shipwreck" not only for individuals but for groups. A therapeutic setting and program is the measure of the environment it takes to struggle against perpetual floundering associated with children's instabilities and variabilities to behave more rationally and responsibly.

Chapter Twelve

University and Community Collaboration

Child Advocacy: A Community Intervention Tactic

When the child advocacy movement is seen as a community intervention tactic, it establishes alternatives for a population of children, where alternatives do not exist, in those structures and processes of child settings and systems of child care which interact with problem development and deviancy careers in children.

The position that this approach takes is that the compelling niche-oriented pressure of the environment and its systems interacts with individual and group vulnerability characteristics to provide deviance careers in children. Child maladaptation is viewed as a transaction between vulnerable children and active labeling and segregating patterns in environments.

Using the above premise, the following sequence will develop a Child Advocacy training compact between a university and a city or community. With this approach a substantial content base and a tradition for continuing growth and evolution must be built into the program for maximum benefit to the child and the community.

As viewed in this context, *advocacy is a community intervention tactic which establishes alternatives for a child, where alternatives do not ordinarily exist, in those structures and processes of child settings, and systems of child care, which interact with problem development and deviancy careers in children.*

Advocacy provides the child and/or his guardian an opportunity to participate in choice and decision through the creation and delineation of alternative structures or processes at each critical point in the child's career.

Child maladaptation or deviation is an interaction between vulnerability characteristics in specific child populations and ecological traps in the environment which come together to shape deviancy careers. Maladaptation is a transaction between vulnerable children and active labeling and segregating patterns in environments.

Environmental "track" or slot pressures (the compelling niche-oriented pressure of the environment and its system) interact with individual and group vulnerability characteristics to produce deviancy careers in children.

The provision of alternatives for children in child settings and child systems, where alternatives do not ordinarily exist, can be accomplished without a theoretical framework. What is important is to develop a community awareness and willingness to make this effort. It is important to orient child services, agencies, and settings to this point of view, and to develop measures whereby a large variety of community members (professionals and other citizens) can play the role of advocate. Unless the settings and systems of child control and influence in a community become receptive to, and initiating of, alternatives to their systematic, niche-imposing actions, advocacy will create conflict and resistance rather than assistance to children.

For this reorientation, a major university and community effort must be made. The strategy is an action-training strategy and has been deliberately offered because of the principle of "psychic persistence" which makes change in communities and individuals so difficult. Psychic persistence is a facet of the socio-cultural resistance to change and must be influenced before existing patterns of thought about children can be altered.

Intrusions from outside the community usually encounter this resistance or psychic persistence. Frequently, when an outside agent enters a community with a goal of change, merger of resources, or new inputs of expert knowledge, there is a subtle closing of ranks against him. He may be tolerated temporarily if he brings extra funds, but even this tolerance frequently lasts only as long as the extra funds are there. When the outsider manages to successfully attach himself to an existing community system, he has usually co-opted to the long-standing traditions of the community's way of doing things. Thus he no longer can be seen as a change agent, but rather one to maintain the status quo.

It seems important to choose a strategy that aims to reach down into the socio- cultural sub-strata of change. In this case Education *is the chosen strategy.* Education *is and has been the only non-violent avenue available to communities for changing both the custom carriers and the customs of the child settings and sub-systems which has been used by societies over the centuries to renew or develop themselves.*

Even with the past experience of using education as the strategy for change, we need to learn to forge an amalgamation of educational tools with community child-rearing actions and to teach others what we learn so that the efforts put forth will not be wasted.

The university and community collaboration project is a three-pronged, inter-related training system of Child Advocacy that can be planned as part of a major training effort. Included, as parts of the project, are two complementary tasks involving environmental simulation and research/development. These complementary efforts are perceived as a single pattern for implementation of the overall action-training strategy.

The major aim of the overall training system is to develop a training compact and a Training Consortium between a university and a community for the immediate purpose of:

- uniting the resources of the university and the community to create an institutional force and institutional structures within child sub-systems and settings of the community that will improve and influence the way the community affects children.

And for the long-range purpose of:

- contributing to a permanent child-advocacy tradition with a developing philosophy, body of knowledge, body of professionals, and a set of techniques in child advocacy.

The initial task would be the development of a training consortium in the community to engage in training university students, and local community agency and citizen personnel in the concepts, attitudes, and methods of child advocacy. A joint faculty can be composed of university, agency, and citizen personnel. Second would be the selection of the community as a basic laboratory tool for child-advocacy as an overall ecological representation of critical forces, agencies, and settings that shape and regulate child behavior in the community.

Lastly, a detailed systems analysis should be conducted in specific child settings and in child sub-systems which sort children into separate tracks. This systematic approach shall be recognized as *mapping career deviance and vulnerable children*. This effort will follow the traces in the environment and its sub-systems that have compelling influences upon the deviance "careers" of vulnerable children. The systems analysis of such ecological traps will try to specify the stages by which children are moved to a specific label and status, extruded from community mainstreams (such as regular classrooms), and placed in segregated niches such as special classes, prisons, correctional units, etc.

The specific strategy recommended to accomplish the above aims is an action-training strategy. This strategy proposes to unite the resources of the community and the university, through a Training Consortium, to improve the way the community influences and services children. This strategy also utilizes the reality circumstances of the community and its child settings and agencies to influence the way university faculty and students learn child-advocacy.

The Training Consortium can be made up of community and university personnel and citizens who will learn from and teach each other. This consortium will seek progressive intensification of the involvement of both parties (university and community) in the lives of children. It will seek to make child-advocacy training a way of life in the community; that is, training, experimentation, and evaluation will become part and parcel of the critical environmental settings and sub-systems serving children.

The training consortium can be constituted from:

- the multi-disciplinary staff and students of a university;
- community representatives from city or community's official agencies; or,
- representation from indigenous populations and the consumers of services or their representatives

The university personnel will represent the university in the Consortium while the city usually hosts a large number of agencies serving children. Thus the Office of Community Relations operating under the supervision of the City Manager can assume the role of coordinator of, or mediator between, these agencies. It is through this office that representatives of these official agencies shall be appointed to the committees guiding the Training Consortium.

Various interest blocs within the community such as the Welfare Rights Mothers, the Neighborhood Community Action Agency Council, and the Citizens' Advisory Council to the schools have been identified. Representatives from this "grass roots" level will also be appointed through the city's Community Relations Office. Community, faculty, and students represented in the Consortium will consist of agency personnel at various levels, paraprofessionals, and parents as interested community lay persons

The faculty of the Training Consortium can consist of university members and community personnel. The faculty will have a changing membership of supervisory teaching, and community agent staff. "Teaching" staff will consist of university faculty, child service staff of community agencies, agency constituency, members of community organizations, community youth, vested-interest group members, etc.

Supervisory staff will consist of both university faculty and appropriate staff personnel of specific school or agency facilities in which university students are placed. Apprenticeship modeling will also be provided university and community students by community-indigenous "child advocates."

The child training effort in the community will be carried out through a variety of training vehicles such as:

- Periodical, scheduled, Child Development and Child Advocacy Training Conferences in the community and the university for Board members, executive personnel, community services aides, parents, civic groups, etc.

- Continuing education in child development and child advocacy for school and agency personnel in the community. This may involve in-service training, it may involve extension courses, it may involve teach-in programs, on-the-job training and classes, it may involve agency process seminar, it may involve tandem-training with university students.

- Pre-service training and in-service training of support personnel such as teaching- aides, outreach workers, etc.

- Placement of university students either in interdisciplinary teams of uni-disciplinary training fellows in a variety of child service systems and child settings in the community.

- Consultation-training from teams or individual university faculty and students of many disciplines offering consultation in child development, development disturbances, child advocacy to child services, and child settings in the community.

- Consultation to the university in child courses, seminars, etc., by community agents, and community service personnel.

There can be numerous university trainees from the multiple disciplines (Social Work, Nursing, Pediatrics, Nutrition, etc.) who have field placements in the community, through the city or community's Field Station. However, the specific student stipends necessary in this plan will provide a new, unique training program for doctoral and post-doctoral students from at least three fields (e.g., psychology, education, and public health). These students will be specifically trained in Child Advocacy and will learn and use specific community practice skills in the community.

The trainees can spend from one to two years (depending on their backgrounds and experiences) twenty hours per week in the Child Advocacy program. The other twenty hours per week will be in their departments taking courses paralleling the community skill training that they will learn and practice in the community. Instead of training each pre-professional disciplinary student only within his own specific technique (e.g., special education, diagnosis and treatment, social casework, legal-aid, etc.), a supplementary body of commonly shared, community-oriented, intervention theory and technology can be taught and practiced jointly by multiple disciplines across service-agency boundaries. This commonly shared body of intervention theory and technology come together naturally to provide a substantive base for the public practice of child advocacy. This body involves:

- consultation theory and practice;
- community and systems organization theory and practice;
- program and environmental planning and development;
- naturalistic research and evaluation; and,
- group dynamic training theory and practice.

This body of human intervention theory and technology has an extensive literature in education, mental health, social work, religion, public health, psychology, law, etc. All of these various disciplines will be in training at the university and in the community. In the public practice of child advocacy each of these disciplines will have to use the skills of this composite body of community intervention knowledge.

As a unified and independent body of knowledge and technology this composite (unlike specific disciplinary techniques such as education, diagnosis and treatment, etc.) is applicable across community structures and community services. The technology not only applies in the realm of general community dynamics, but to every human service system of the community, including:

- education and its school systems;
- health and its clinics, hospitals, etc.;
- welfare and its social service systems;
- corrections and its judicial, detention and correction systems; and,
- religion and its churches.

The functioning community provides the only viable, unified constellation of settings for such training. The forces of the community which influence child care in the school are the same forces which influence child care in hospitals and clinics, etc. The neighborhoods that produce high rates of developmental disabilities also produce high rates of delinquency, health problems, etc. The economic, governmental, and special interest power forces which shape programs in the social services department also shape special classes in the school system.

The agency and their service delivery patterns (schools, welfare departments, juvenile facilities, etc.) form an interrelated set of social institutions that support and supplement the family as the developmental agents of society. Their interrelationship and the necessity for harmonizing and orchestrating their actions and effects upon individual children and special populations of children can only be learned through training that integrates experiences across agency settings.

Each trainee will become a staff member of the Field Station and will share responsibility for the overall functioning of the Field Station in the area of Child Advocacy. He/she will participate in the Environmental Simulation Task and in the research and developmental task of mapping child deviancy careers. His/her dissertation or thesis in his/her academic program will be related to one of these tasks. Each student will be assigned a special interest community bloc to help organize that bloc around child advocacy and to help that particular special interest group utilize the training resources of the Field Station. The trainee will also be assigned to provide staff functions for the Child Advocacy Task Force of the Advocacy Committee. In addition he/she will have an assignment to a specific system or agency of the community (education, mental health, Corrections, etc.).

The trainees who will have child advocacy training stipends provided through this proposed project will participate in two major seminars:

- A Child Advocacy Seminar: (other students of university will be admitted to this seminar). This seminar will be devoted to child advocacy efforts and methods taking place in this country. They will learn about the recent use of law in the United States in special education and other areas, as an advocacy strategy for children.

- A Public Practice Seminar: The trainee will participate in a continuing community-process seminar built around the student's activities in his public-practice practica. The faculty will be multiple disciplines, both university and community. The seminar will be modeled after "Grand Rounds" in medical settings, where students in community training will present their "case" material (e.g., consultation, community organization, etc.) and review the literature related to the critical aspects of their "case." The combined faculty and other students would then critique the presentation.

All of the trainees' experiences will be under close supervision. In many cases there may be double supervision; that is, direct field supervision by the agency personnel in the agency in which the student is placed, and didactic supervision by the university faculty. Supervision will be oriented to *Advocacy*. It will be slanted toward selecting and advocating for specific populations of children who need professional advocates.

There is a general experience for students which can help them understand the fractional nature of agency functioning and the diverse points of view which different agencies have with regard to services and service needs. This general training method involves Community Rounds which sets up planned experiences where students accompany welfare workers, probation officers, police, public health nurses, and other personnel on their service rounds. This can provide the opportunity to examine the way in which each agent group conceptualized human problems and brings its agency service to bear upon the problems. Each has its own perspective on human behavior. Each picks out a special segment of behavior to which it addresses itself. Each has a different idea of what needs to be done in intervention into the problem. These diverse points of view and methods need to be conceptualized in an overall perspective by the student.

The paradigm presents the total child advocacy training system as it is projected. The City Field Station at the apex of the paradigm is the locational focus of the project and the housing facility for the Task Force of the advocacy project. The central staff of the Child Advocacy Project located in the Field Station, together with two advisory bodies, will be the Child Advocacy Task Force in the Field Station. The central staff will consist of:

- the Field Station Director; and
- the Coordinator of Child Advocacy Studies.

This central staff will be given principal guidance by two organizational bodies:

An executive committee: This executive committee will consist of three to five members of the university faculty, and three to five members from community residents. The community members will also be an advisory group to the Office of Community Relations in the City Manager's Office. One or two members of the executive committee will be appointed from representatives of the poor, and/or constituency groups of existing agencies. These will be people such as an articulate welfare mother from the Welfare Rights Committee, and an elected representative of youth from the city's youth's organizations

Standing community interest blocs: The Bloc Committees will represent the natural special interest blocs who influence child growth and development in the city. Stipend-paid trainees under the supervision of faculty will be assigned responsibility for organizing and assisting each bloc.

There will eventually be quite a number of such community blocs. The purpose of such interest blocs will be to assist the

Field Station Director, his staff, and the Executive Child Advocacy Committee in assuring Child Advocacy training for community members within their bloc of interest, to assist in gaining entry into their population, to plan training programs and provide teaching resources from within their group, and to help in obtaining necessary funds for child advocacy studies and training within their group. Possible student blocs could be:

Multi-problem neighborhood populations

- A neighborhood containing the poorest sections of housing in the city, predominantly dilapidated, low-income housing, and poor living conditions might be selected

A public housing project is a center for petty crime and other conditions found in high-risk neighborhoods.

Youth Organizations

Special Representation Groups

Planning and Coordinating Bodies

- United Community Services Planning Division

- Regional Planning Commission

- Cooperative Area Manpower Planning System

- Comprehensive Health Planning Council

- Regional Interagency Committee on Mental Health Planning Council

- Community Mental Health Services Board

- Regional Council on Law Enforcement and Criminal Justice

Government and City Management

- The city operates under a Commissioner-Management system of government. The mayor and commissioners, part-time officials, are elected while career appointees staff the various branches of government with the City

Manager serving as Chief Administrator. The Community Relations Department is directly responsible to the City Manager.

Professional Guilds

- County Education Association
- County Bar Association
- County Medical Association

Official Agencies

- Social-Welfare:

  Parochial Social Services

  Family Service and Children's Aid

  County Department of Social Services

  United Community Services

- Correctional:

  County Juvenile Detention Home

  City Police Department

  County Juvenile Court

- Educational:

  County Intermediate School District

  City Public Schools

- Medical

  Mental Health Center

The university should develop a training-reference community for its ecologically-oriented training. A staff person spends full time in the Field Station dividing his/her time between community and university offices. In addition, the Director named in this project is spending organizational time in the Field Station.

The Field Station as a unit of university should be a linking structure between the university and the community. One of its major purposes is to provide semi-protected training for many disciplines in reality settings for children, as these settings are constantly undergoing the dynamic press of myriad community forces.

The Field Station, as a linking structure between the university and the community provides potential access to:

- The formal power structures of the community (the government structures, designated Boards and Councils, controllers of industry, and economy of the community).

- The child-rearing institutions, agencies and facilities (education, judicial-corrections, religious, social welfare, mental health, etc.).

- The informal force-units of the community that directly influence children's lives and children's programs (parent pressure groups, militant action groups, drug-user groups, "hard hat" groups, etc.).

- Natural behavior settings for special populations of children. (For instance, play settings, neighborhood settings, street corner settings, and home settings of "ghetto" children).

A conscious organizational effort to develop access to the total child behavioral field of special cultural samples (i.e., inner city crisis ghetto, rural agricultural, sub-community, suburban bedroom sub-community, university fringe group, and hippie sub-community). The trainee will be able to immerse himself/herself in a particular sample culture and become a participant/observer of child behavior in its living context. He/she will have the opportunity to design and implement naturalistic studies and interventions fitted to the particular child environment and the particular population of the unique cultural group he/she is studying.

Aside from any value that may accrue to the community from the training program itself, it is expected that the university reciprocity could consist of:

- Additional "staff" in undermanned agencies in the form of placement of numbers of students from various professional disciplines.

- In order to arrange release time for agency or school personnel in the community, trainees will assume the functions and roles of community staff personnel whenever this personnel participates in training.

- Consultation services of multiple disciplines and professionals where there may be a lack or shortage of such personnel...particularly in undermanned settings.

- Special extension courses may be arranged for college credit where there are enough agency or school staff to justify such credit courses.

- Additional "outreach" trainees who could work at the neighborhood level under the auspices of existing undermanned agencies.

In this Child Advocacy model, an action-training strategy has been chosen as the most likely strategy to influence the psycho-cultural and socio-cultural substrata of the community and its child care systems.

This strategy has been chosen also because it seems necessary to build a body of knowledge in the child-advocacy field and to inculcate this orientation and body of knowledge in a cadre of professionals who can carry it to other locations and train other professionals to focus their careers around Child Advocacy. The university's multi-disciplinary training resources and its community Field Station seems a logical locus of this strategy.

The timing of this effort seems appropriate to the new pressures for community-related training and community participation among the students in various professional schools and departments. Students from among many disciplinary training programs at the university can view the Field Station as a choice training site.

The design of the overall Child Advocacy training system involves three major complementary tasks:

- Establishing a university-community Training Consortium in Child Advocacy through a training-reference community. This Training Consortium will be independent of any particular agency or vested interest group of the community, and any particular school or department of the university.

The focal vehicle for generating, consolidating and staffing this Training Consortium is a Task Force in the Field Station. This task force will be guided by a community and university Executive Committee, and advised by various special interest blocs in the community. It will be staffed by:

- a joint community-university faculty;
- a coordinator of community studies;
- five trainees in the public practice of Child Advocacy, who will be training and implementing the Child Advocacy action-training strategy.

In addition, staff and students from numerous disciplines in the institute for the university will work through the Field Station to provide training, service, and research functions in many agencies and special interest blocs throughout the community.

The Child Advocacy trainees who will receive stipends will spend twenty hours per week in the Child Advocacy training program. They will:

- be assigned to carefully designed and supervised practica experiences in consultation, organization, naturalistic research and evaluation, training, and group dynamic skills;
- assist in data collection in the Environmental Simulation Task and the Career Tracking Task;
- be assigned to organize and provide staff assistance to one of the special interest blocs;

- provide direct staff assistance to individual members of the Child Advocacy Executive Committee in the Field Station.

In addition, they will participate in a Child Advocacy Seminar and a Public Practice Seminar.

A wide range of training activities will be developed in the community. Such child advocacy training will include in-service training, special conferences, extension courses, consultations, etc., within, between, and among agencies (e.g., education, social services, health, and corrections), and special interest blocs. These Child Advocacy training activities will be woven together into a single community curriculum coordinated through the Field Station and the Child Advocacy Task Force.

The other two tasks involved in the Child Advocacy Training System are:

Simulation Laboratory in which a simulation will be developed to reflect the child settings, forces, and agencies of the community. Such simulations have been developed and have become successful training vehicles for the Center for Disease Control of the U.S. Public Health Department, and the Environmental Simulation Laboratory of the University of Michigan.

Deviancy Career Tracking. This will be a research and development aspect of the Child Advocacy Training System. It will rely heavily upon systems analysis, naturalistic research methodology and epidemiological and ecological research methods.

Source: Dr. William Rhodes provided this advocacy design in a proposal (grant-in-aid) in 1969, Bureau of Education for the Handicapped, requesting funds to develop a community-university based child advocacy program. Dr. Rhodes is an internationally known clinical psychologist and was on the faculty of Peabody College, Vanderbilt University, served in the National Institute of Mental Health and University of Michigan. Dr. Rhodes is now visiting professor at the University of South

Florida, Tampa, Florida. The authors have summarized Dr. Rhodes' main ideas into the proceeding format.

Chapter Thirteen

A Parent Training Approach

Many investigations in the past decades have examined the growth and development of children as related to the influences of parents and their child-rearing activities. Highly trained professionals in all the behavioral sciences have become quite involved in studies and treatment of children. Billions of dollars are earmarked for education, mental health, health, vocational, occupational, and correctional systems, yet limited amounts have been allocated to the parent rearing practices as they affect vulnerable children. What has come forth in the literature concerning the influence of the parents and their child rearing activities has been punctuated with huge gaps in the theories, programs and empirical data concerning the impact of social structure, physical environments, cultural values, and practices relative to children's learning, achievement, socialization, and feelings. We continue to fill correctional programs with our children and youth; stack our unnecessary centers and hospitals with mentally ill and retarded youngsters; lose children who fail in school and drop out, and those who commit offenses against school, which precipitate their expulsion.

Children are becoming more and more violent and estranged. Is it true that institutions, which serve children, are failing and are no longer responsive and effective in the education, treatment, and care of children? It appears so! We continue to support programs of the organization and bureaucracy that purport to serve children while, at the same time, ignoring the real and tragic circumstances surrounding children's lives. Financial investments into programs very often are a blind man's approach to critical issues in providing services to children. Global and non-analytic research on poverty, social class, youth culture, urban-rural influence, and socio-economic status are insufficient. It is becoming more apparent that the main reason for this insufficient reporting is that the objectives do not reflect any more or relevant interactive influences on children's behavior and overall development. Research about the various frameworks of how, where and why children grow and develop a certain way, critical to the issues of understanding deviance, is left to the imagination or conjecture.

Institutions must become more responsive to the needs of children, to change as the problems change, to care and share responsibility for failure when a child has not succeeded, and to have effective ways to act to correct that situation. We cannot expect our children to become mature citizens who will feel accountable to a system whose basic institutions have failed to be accountable to their needs for learning and support as children. A personal investment is required of all citizens, professionals, and laymen who share, with children and youth, responsibility for goals and programs. That decision cannot be left solely to bureaucrats. Problems of children cannot be fully responded to until we have seen the problems through the eyes of children. This cannot be done until we get involved with children and that means learning to ask them where it hurts, not telling them (Smith, 1997).

Child advocacy should link the home, the school, the neighborhood, and the communities to ensure the children's needs are met. A community-based approach is needed to ensure that children get the services they need through holding child-serving agencies accountable in this matter; assisting agencies to work cooperatively for children; maintaining children in the normal community settings to the fullest extent possible; and, finally, recognizing that parents and families are invariably the best advocates for their own children (Paul, Neufeld, & Pelosi, 1977; Smith, 1997).

Evidence that the well being of the child is highly related to the well being of his family suggests a need for an advocacy program that includes the family as well as the child. Splitting of services by planning for child services apart from the needs of the family probably has limited usefulness. Relative to a family and child advocacy program, professionals should use their skills to support family and community responsibility and control. In the current approach to child services, the professionals, agencies, and institutions assume most or all of the responsibility and control without adequate representation of the families and communities who have a stake in program and service outcomes (Paul, Neufeld & Pelosi, 1977; Reay, 1996).

This approach could be defined as a consumer-controlled outreach system with two major objectives:

- To obtain more responsive, adequate and effective service from child and family service agencies.
- To develop the strengths, skills and initiatives of families and communities to solve their own problems.

Essential elements of this approach would include:

- Analysis of the needs of children, families and the community, and development of a system of human services.
- Emphasis on family-centered preventive programs oriented to health, education and welfare.

A council of parents and community leaders who could employ professional staff to operate the program could direct this kind of program. The director could employ a staff of family and child consultants to lead small teams of family and child advocates working directly with families. These families and child consultants might be indigenous paraprofessionals whose training would be based on an academic career ladder model

(North Carolina Governor's Advocacy Commission, 1974, and National Mental Health Association and the Federation of Families for Children's Mental Health, 1993). Ideal would be a parity that would develop between a university training program and community and state resources. The goal of this alliance would be to accomplish the training necessary for implementation of the program.

The target groups in the community are its child-serving agencies and settings. These groups would become the forum to influence and determine the procedures for the training staff and parent-trainees to learn about child advocacy. The staff of a local advocacy group, university staff, student-parent interns, and representatives could provide the coordination of resources from the community's child serving agencies. The teaching and supervising staff should be selected from institutions of higher education, from select child agency staff, members of community organizations and other relevant community groups closest to experimental and pilot project communities.

The training should be a major continuing concern of the Child Advocacy Board (local and state) in liaison with the institutions of higher education and with relevant community agency representatives. The new kinds of child advocacy workers would be trained to work directly with families and children, with community organizations, child development agencies, or in a consultation capacity.

More precisely, the child advocacy training effort in the community would be carried out through a variety of training delivery systems to include:

- Well-planned, periodical community training sessions on child development and child advocacy, organized for the leadership personnel in select community child-serving agencies, civic groups, and select natural advocates such as parents and paraprofessionals. The local advocacy staff in cooperation with university personnel would see these training sessions as their prime responsibility along with the organizational work of developing child advocacy.

- Continuing education in child development and child advocacy for the major child- serving agency personnel such as welfare, school, educational, and correctional personnel. Since this approach could involve in-service training, extension course work, and teach-in programs, the university staff would assume more responsibility for this work.

- Parent-students interning specifically in child advocacy would be placed in teams of child-serving agencies in the community. The institutions of higher education would be responsible for training and overall coordination in this instance.

- The local advocacy staff as consultants would take major responsibility for training and visits to experimental programs; the purpose of consultation would be to focus on child development, child deviance, and child advocacy (Paul, Neufeld & Pelosi, 1977; Smith, 1997).

The trainees should be constituted from groups of natural child advocates, citizens, and professional personnel associated with children. They should be trained on the job in the community as well as at specifically organized, periodic sessions. The training will focus on learning to use specific advocacy practices and skills in the community.

The "course work" approach to the training will cover several broad areas and will not duplicate existing training and professional or allied experiences of the "trainees." Information and knowledge that cuts across discipline and focuses on children's interests and needs will compromise part of the course work. Interaction techniques should comprise another part.

The course work should include areas such as:

- Child Development

- Child Advocacy
- Community Organization
- Program Planning and Development
- Research and Evaluation
- Consultation Theory and Practice
- Group Work and Dynamics

These areas are but a few that can be mentioned.

Trainees could be trained within these broad areas to fulfill very precise roles.

Some personnel would be trained to work with families and children, others with community agencies, others with the eco-political community system, while others would be trained to work specifically in schools, institutions, and other such child-serving agencies.

The community selected to participate in experimental child advocacy projects would be the training setting for the development and implementation of child advocacy. The community harbors the child-serving agencies that are essentially a part of the community. The community needs to engage in procedures and activities to hold such child-serving agencies accountable to the community and to the children they purport to serve. The values and behavior that influence the lives of children are ones that not only permeate the agencies but are also alive in the community at large. Child advocacy would not only be interested in the micro-culture of child-serving agencies and what they do or do not do to children, but would further examine the micro-culture of the community to determine the inter-relatedness of influences, forces, values, etc., that influence the lives of children. Therefore, child advocacy, as proposed here, wishes to investigate the phenomenon of childcare and services through the broad social, political, and professional attitudes ranging from the family, child settings and to the community itself.

Because the advocacy approach to meeting children's needs is relatively new, few people have been trained to use it. Local and statewide advocacy groups should assume responsibility to effect more and better quality services to improve the lives of children. These groups can establish a priority for programs of continuing education and in-service training for personnel to assume child advocacy roles.

Other appropriate training activities may include:

- Continuing education and in-service training programs in child advocacy organized by mental health centers, centers for the mentally retarded, correctional institutions, and other service-oriented and community-based programs serving children.

- Development of "do-it-yourself" training packages for use by various parents, social, fraternal, and professional groups active in community affairs.

- Support workshops and institutes to increase the readiness of people already working in child-serving capacities, such as doctors, public health nurses, teachers, lawyers, policemen, clergy, and welfare workers to include child advocacy among their activities.

Here we are trying to establish the essential components of a system of child advocacy, emphasizing the role of parents and family involvement. In addition, a cooperative venture facilitating both universities and state and community resources to become active in a training procedure designed to advocate for children is proposed. A program such as the one described could lead to the development of viable arrangements within the family and community to mediate child-parent discord, child-school failure, and child-neighborhood difficulties. This sort of approach could develop a collective concern about child development in a given family and neighborhood, become a vehicle for parent education, and support parent involvement in meeting children's needs (Tompkins, Brooks, & Dorne, 1977).

Chapter Fourteen

A Model Program: Child Advocacy Commission

City of Durham, North Carolina

The Child Advocacy Commission of Durham (CACD) is a non-profit organization formed in 1973 to speak out on behalf of children in Durham and surrounding counties. Since 1976 the Commission has received funds from the County to assist in its mission. Funding also comes from the United Way and the Junior League, as well as individual contributors. A 15-member Board of citizens from around the Triangle area including Durham, Chapel Hill, and Raleigh, North Carolina governs the Commission. The Commission recognizes that many of Durham's children have unmet special needs, are at risk of abuse and neglect, live in poverty, and have unstable home lives placing them at risk for adolescent problems or simply falling through the cracks. Further, economic conditions, substance abuse, a high divorce rate, and stress have split up families leaving children in vulnerable situations. The Commission offers families and children a legal advocacy service to help with legal matters or to improve services or relations within the families and/or protect the interests and welfare of the children. The Commission also provides community education programs for parents, professionals, civic groups, churches, and corporations to address issues facing children and families (CACD, 1997, p. 1).

The Commission serves children primarily from poor, working poor, and lower-middle class families. They currently serve over 600 families per year with only one attorney. The majority of the cases are referrals from the Durham County Public Schools System, and the Durham County Department of Social Services Child Support Section. These two sources account for over one-half of the cases. The remainder comes from the North Carolina Legal Assistance Program, Clerks of Court, Durham County staff, and word of mouth. The Child Advocacy Commission provides community education to parents, professionals, and students in hopes of making all citizens more aware of the problems facing children and families. This also includes a rapid response team on the Board to respond to legislative issues impacting children. This rapid response allows for mass faxes to be delivered to interested parties alerting them to the impact on the children and encouraging them to respond proactively (CACD, 1997, p. 2).

Objectives:

- To facilitate improvement to the total health and welfare of all children.

- To function as a clearing house for addressing problems of Durham's children.

- To serve as a referral service to agencies working with the children, thereby assuring prompt and thorough treatment.

- To assist agencies in the sharing of information and co-operation for treatment of children.

- To consult with agencies, public officials, and private citizens in order to improve awareness of issues impacting children.

Things are not going well for many of our youth. There are children in Durham who come from homes and families that cannot provide for their physical, intellectual, and emotional well being. For these young persons the legal, health, social, and educational systems in our community become their primary opportunity for growth and development.

Serious problems in Durham include:

- Children and youth experiencing physical and emotional abuse at home and elsewhere.

- A high number of youth coming to the attention of juvenile law enforcement and court officials every year.

- A significant number of young people who are expelled, suspended, or truant from school, and who drop out without achieving academic or employment skills.

- Infants and children who lack proper health care, mental health services, adequate diet, housing and clothing.

- A teenage pregnancy rate that continues to be of great concern and cost to the community.

Children are our youngest citizens, but they are also the future of Durham. Child advocacy ensures that the needs of children and youth are considered a priority in planning and allocation of resources. Durham has a responsibility to its children. The community as a whole will benefit from coordinated efforts to assure that our children can become healthy, productive adults (CACD, 1997, p. 3).

The Advocacy Commission speaks and acts for children and youth who otherwise would have no strong voice on their behalf. The Commission works to ensure that children's needs are met such that they are able to grow and develop their full individual potential.

The Legal Services offered focus on:

- Mediation and counseling on child custody and child support issues.

- Legal assistance to children in need of substitute parental care because of abuse, neglect, dependency, divorce, emotional problems, and other family difficulties (custody, adoption, termination of parental rights).
- Representation of children as their guardian ad litem in difficult divorce and custody matters in District Court.
- Representation as guardian ad litem in criminal matters in which they are the victim of physical or sexual abuse.
- Representation of children in administrative hearings to secure appropriate services.
- Representation of children in District Court who have been categorized as delinquent.
- Representation of children who have been suspended or expelled from public schools.

Profile of Typical Cases:

- A grandmother seeking custody of grandchildren who are at risk because of parental neglect.
- A parent seeking an advocate for a child who has behavior problems at school and needs appropriate services.
- A parent/guardian seeking an advocate for a child charged with a crime.
- A relative seeking custody of a child due to any number of reasons (i.e., to get the child in school, or the child running away from an abusive home).
- A father or a mother of a child seeking to mediate a dispute over custody of the child.
- A social worker from the County Department of Social Services seeking assistance in resolving a family dispute over an at-risk child.
- A school counselor seeking assistance in helping a student or in helping to resolve family disputes.

- A juvenile court counselor seeking assistance with a child charged in committing a crime.

The Commission works in coordination with the local inter-agency task force on juvenile justice that meets monthly to discuss coordination of services among the various local agencies. The focus of this task force is children who are hard to place or difficult to obtain services for. Members of this task force are put together by the Commission and consist of persons from the Department of Social Services, Juvenile Services, Duke University "Back on Track" Program, Substance abuse, Maternal Health, Edgemont Community Center, and Durham Public Schools.

The Commission also is active partners with area law schools by offering internships for law students. This affords students a hands-on opportunity to be a part not only of the legal system, but to see the overall impact on society of children in need and in trouble.

The Commission is also engaged in innovative public awareness programs. In 1997, working in collaboration with N.C. Public Allies, a non-profit group that places young people in apprenticeship, they will unveil a documentary which puts a face on the children of the Triangle (Cities in Durham, Chapel Hill, and Raleigh) and the problems they face. This documentary will be viewed at a public celebration, and videotapes will be made available to schools, churches and community organizations (CACD, 1997, p. 2).

The unique aspect of the Child Advocacy Commission is that while many children's groups provide much-needed advocacy and policy analysis, the Commission focuses on providing this direct legal representation to children who otherwise would fall through the cracks or receive less customized care through a court-appointed attorney. Without the Commission, many children and families would have nowhere to go, and would continue in untenable circumstances, or be caught in the system in which they do not have adequate representation.

The focus by the Commission on mediation also saves many county and local dollars, as these disputes can be solved outside the already overburdened court systems.

In summary, the job of CACD is to assure that all agencies and systems serving children are meeting the needs of Durham youth and providing services effectively. The advocacy approach is to facilitate interagency planning and collaboration both for individual children (case advocacy) and for groups of children (class advocacy). Advocacy accomplishes this by:

- encouraging child-serving agencies to be responsive to Durham children's needs and to coordinate services with other agencies;

- monitoring service delivery and assessing needs;

- fostering communication and coordination among agencies;

- helping to develop new and existing resources;

- providing information and referral resource counseling and individual case advocacy services to children and their families; and,

- monitoring legislation affecting children and families.

(CACD, 1997, p. 3).

The CACD provides action for children and youth who otherwise have no strong voice. Child advocacy works to improve the lives of children and to ensure those children are able to grow and develop to their full potential. Child advocacy is committed to the belief that all children have the right to a safe, nurturing environment and the right to love (CACD, 1997, p. 3).

Chapter Fifteen

Pathways to Develop Local Advocacy Councils

There are five priorities in the pathway to develop local advocacy councils. These five priorities are:

- development of advocacy councils;
- development of a political constituency;
- promotion of a review of existing service delivery patterns;
- promotion of public information and public relations; and,
- assurance of accountability.

Priority I: Development of Advocacy Councils

Need

Provides a conceptual and structural umbrella program (parent council) under which to examine and resolve a variety of problems related to the provisions of better services at the local level.

Goal

Development of local advocacy councils in cooperation with parent, civic, youth, and professional groups throughout the designated area.

Ultimate Benefits

Creation of support structures closely related to home, community, and school activities through a neighborhood, community, or county advocacy system that will facilitate the child's acquisition and application of skills to maximize his/her potential. Support of the development of an environment within neighborhoods, communities, and counties that is supportive of and responsive to children's needs.

Strategies (For Parent Council)

Administrative

- Review literature and legislation and consult with persons within and outside designated area who are currently engaged in research, conceptualization, and application of advocacy principles to develop models and procedures for establishing local advocacy councils.

- Contact and meet parent, civic, and professional groups who, through survey, express interest in establishing local advocacy in their respective districts.

- Develop a speaker's bureau comprised of interested parties who could be called upon on a rotating basis to fill speaking engagements throughout the designated area to increase awareness of advocacy.

- Organize a conference to:

- Review procedures for establishing advocacy councils.
- Develop an association of local advocacy councils that will serve as a vehicle for communicating, exchanging ideas, planning, and sharing resources and expertise among the different local advocacy councils.

Programmatic

- Assist local advocacy councils to:
  - Identify individuals who are not receiving needed services.
  - To provide data indicating how service denial occurred and disseminate the information to the community, as a first step to developing remedial measures.
  - Identify local services that could respond to the individual needs in the community.
  - Use the data gathered above to identify a mechanism that will ensure provision of services to all in need.

Priority II: Development of a Political Constituency

Need

A political constituency at local and state levels

Goal

Promotion of a political organization

Ultimate Benefits

Effective collective measures – e.g., support for the modification of state agency policies and development of legislation – to increase the services and attitudes necessary to assist everyone to achieve his/her fullest potential. Establishment and maintenance of inter-organizational coordination of all civic, parent, and governmental groups advocating for children.

Strategy

A strategy would be developed for bringing together representatives of special interest advocacy groups to identify concerns and discuss objectives and ways of meeting them. Meetings and conferences would be held with advocacy groups and government and legislative officials at state and national levels to discuss the establishment of policies and programs to further the interests of children.

Priority III: Promotion of a Review of Existing Service Delivery Patterns

Need:

A thorough review of statutes and policies determining state-level provision of existent services and programs, and an assessment of efforts to implement that which is mandated by law.

Goal

Understanding (as a result of accurate documentation) of the legal basis for the provision of services at the state level as a basis for ensuring accountability and development of action plans to increase service delivery.

Ultimate Benefits

Preservation and growth of programs as mandated by general statutes supporting existing services and delivery patterns.

Strategy

- *Personnel* (staff, consultants and volunteers)
- *Action*
  - Identify and obtain all general statutes and policies governing the provision of state and local therapeutic services and programs.
  - Analyze the provision and prepare a documented report of findings.
  - Conduct site visits with policy and decision-makers and other responsible personnel to determine whether methodologies for providing and delivering services protect the mandated rights of target populations.
  - Document the results of investigations and prepare recommendations to legislative and other officials at federal and state program offices.

Priority IV: Promotion of Public Information and Public Relations

Need

Increased public awareness of the efforts of local advocacy councils.

Goals

Establishment of state and nation public information relations programs which inform and stimulate interest and involvement in advocacy action.

Ultimate Benefits

Public visibility as a way of furthering the mission of the advocacy movement.

- **Information**
  - Issue weekly news releases describing developments in the provision of quality services.
  - Schedule television appearances for a consultant to explore the benefits of establishing advocacy councils and promoting service delivery.

Priority V: Assurance of Accountability

Need

Maintenance of quality service delivery and responsiveness to consumer needs.

Goals

Accountability of service delivery systems and enforcement of legislative mandates.

Ultimate Benefits

A system for guiding the planning and evaluation of service delivery which will lead to adequate attention to consumer.

Strategies

- **Assessment**
  - Determine adequacy of service delivery in institutional and community settings.
  - Determine unserved populations and the reasons for exclusion from or denial of services.
- **Planning/evaluation guidelines:**
  - Develop planning and service delivery evaluation techniques which foster accountability.
  - Utilize the local advisory councils to distribute guidelines to agencies and institutions (Tompkins, 1977).

Chapter Sixteen

Advocacy in the Treatment and Education of Adjudicated Children

Introduction

As the North Carolina Department of Human Resources strives to prevent responsibility for education and treatment programs from being lost in conflicting bureaucratic aims and procedures, it also must not allow valuable programs to falter because of inadequate financial, physical, and human resources. Rather than responding after the fact to crisis, at which point resources are focused on program redirection because of the deficiencies or failures, the development of quality programs should be established as a high priority from the outset. The leadership needs to reach aggressively into its program resources to develop new services and modify existing service components so that the range of services available matches the assessed range of students' needs.

You and I know that the application of the most sophisticated concepts in programs for students is certainly not a magic solution to programming. We acknowledge that there are constantly huge discordant forces at work. For example, a close friend's experience illustrates this point.

111

"On one occasion we set off for camp by bus with a load of very aggressive little youngsters. The group included a little girl who looked like a little angel.

She may have been little, but she was not an angel! Her mother came to send her off and informed her in a loud voice, 'Be sure to be a good girl and mind everything that these nice people tell you.' Then quietly leaning down to the child, she said, 'But remember, you are my daughter and you don't take no shit from nobody.' And I can assure you, she didn't take 'no shit from nobody.' The child was oppositional from the word 'go'."

It is obvious that many students' entry in the Department of Human Resources education and treatment programs is a result of the particular student having been identified as disabled, or some as a result of having been labeled a failure and at risk of pursuing pathological development.

Limitations on our ability to bring about family and social change and to shape the future constitutes our greatest constraint and intensifies the need for our investment in maximizing the benefits for students, many of whom must be specially strengthened for later adaptation for less than ideal situations.

The following recommendations reflect concern that programs be evaluated for accountability and gaps in services be identified and eliminated. The coordination of both the assessment and the delivery of services is essential if we are to avoid duplication and policies which are at cross purposes.

There is a need to establish objectives to:

- determine how priorities for programs are identified and adopted;
- identify areas of importance for student programs that were overlooked in program proposals;
- provide recommendations so that better programs can be planned; and,

- provide recommendations for a more effective review of programs on a regular and continuing basis.

Few of the problems can be identified as momentary, and few have solutions for which a single treatment could provide an instant cure. The problems have a long-range impact on the State of North Carolina. These problems extend back into the past, and stretch into the future. Therefore, careful planning and coordinated efforts are not only desirable, but crucial.

Education and treatment must ultimately aim at providing experiences which strengthen the students' human potential - experiences which, given the essential nature of the student and his human destiny, must be by themselves inherently pleasurable and worthwhile. We emphasize achievement rather than past injury - stressing not so much what the student leaves behind, but what he carries away as his own.

Since one of the major concerns of the North Carolina Department of Human Resources is to encourage and facilitate the improvement in services while preserving the achievements of the past, the current proposed thrust for program and budget analysis can identify several necessary steps in changing programs:

- Construct statements describing the educational and treatment services to be provided in measurable terms.
- Study personnel functions necessary to provide these services.
- Develop evaluation processes to measure the statement of educational and treatment services to be provided against the outcome of administrative and professional input.

This evaluation thrust should result in assessment of outcomes in students' success in achievement, socialization and placement.

Specifically, critics of the current focus in education and treatment of students have pointed out the failure of programs to deal with the "whole" child, including the failure to see academic learning in the larger context of child development, the failure to address crucial socialization and psychosocial needs, and the failure to understand the education and treatment implications of the economic and social environments in which many at-risk students reside.

Many current practices may appear in direct conflict with characteristics of effective schools identified by researchers, including the development of maximum rather than minimum competencies, the concentration of total school energies and resources on basic skill acquisition, the frequent and comprehensive monitoring of student progress, high and increasing levels of staff expectations regarding student achievement, and a collaborative and comprehensive effort by administrators and other educational personnel to improve student skills and socialization.

Our work must be centered on the idea of accountability, whereby we no longer take for granted that merely funding a program or idea will make it work. Our work with students must be productive and yielding results. If it is not, we must be adaptable enough to try something else.

Objectives

In the development of a prototype, futuristic training-correctional programs for delinquent and/or adjudicated children, these main purposes are essential:

- To treat, rehabilitate, and educate very young delinquent and/or adjudicated children.
- To coordinate such treatment, rehabilitation, and education procedures and programs with the major communities in the geographic area, i.e., Raleigh, Durham, and

Chapel Hill for the aim of creating model community-based programs.

- To coordinate all relevant activities of service to children, training of personnel, and research with the major institutions of higher education in the Triangle area.

- To develop model training programs for the variety of professional, paraprofessional, and volunteer personnel to work effectively in training schools, public schools, and community-based programs established to assist delinquent, adjudicated children and to conduct professional development and research in this area.

- To develop a functional system and methodology for evaluating knowledge, attitudes, and skills.

- Recycle trainees back in correctional training and public schools. This program should be implemented in a newly constructed, specially equipped center for children and youth who have problems in academic tasks, human relationships, and self-organization and who are adjudicated. It should emphasize the needs of our very *young* delinquent children.

Locale

The proposed prototype program could be located in the Research Triangle Park, a 5,000 acre location within the Triangle formed by Raleigh, Durham, and Chapel Hill. The Research Park is the home of the Research Triangle Institute, a non-profit corporation which draws on and enriches the University of North Carolina at Chapel Hill; North Carolina State University at Raleigh, and Duke University at Durham, to aid in the provision of research. The proposed location is tangent to schools, communities, mental health-public health clinics, centers, churches, citizen volunteer groups, State Government offices, and so on. The proposed site would be assessable to members of the General Assembly to visit and be briefed on the progress and programs being developed and implemented by the North Carolina Division of Youth Services.

Rationale

Youngsters who are unable to succeed in academic tasks and human relationships have increasingly challenged communities, public schools, and training schools. They very often become anti-social and aggressive. Many of these are very young, pre-adolescent children who are overwhelmed by failure. They fail to:

- achieve academically;
- exercise proper judgment;
- organize their thoughts and energies for constructive activities; and,
- behave in socially acceptable patterns.

They very often wind up in the courts and training schools. These continuing failures isolate them from their peers and alienate them from adults. Without resolution of these problems, many of these young people will return or enter the community with poor vocational preparation and with strong feelings of inadequacy and hostility. Some will withdraw from work or social demands and become additional burdens on their families, communities, and schools which are already under stress.

To prevent some of this waste of human resources, with its heavy cost for the individual and the community, a prototype center for young boys and girls with special needs is proposed for the Triangle area in North Carolina.

Need Assessment

The Division of Youth Services can establish the feasibility of initiating a model prototype service, demonstration, training and research center for our adjudicated young children. The Division of Youth Services can establish and defend its position that there is a high priority and need for:

- Early identification, diagnosis, and remediation within public schools, training schools, and communities to improve performance of children with adjustment and learning problems and who have been adjudicated.

- To develop a center program for treatment, rehabilitation, and education for the evaluation and adjustment of delinquent young boys and girls in three types of settings:

  - *Training schools*

  - *Public schools*

  - *Community-based programs*

- To train professional, paraprofessional, and volunteers to effectively work with delinquent children in the variety of settings noted previously.

- To research and evaluate services and training approaches to develop model and workable programs for such children found in all settings.

Proposed Center

The proposal suggests the development of this program in the Triangle area to initiate, develop, and implement a prototype program having access to every conceivable resource available such as institutions of higher education, public schools, health and mental health centers, communities, and so on. The goal of the center is to move children back into communities, to train personnel, and research areas relevant to the treatment, rehabilitation, and education of young delinquent children.

Project Prototype Development

Representative personnel around the State and Department of Corrections/Division of Youth Services in the Department of Human Resources and allied governmental agencies could serve on planning committees including teachers, counselors, psychologists, administrators, supervisors, representatives from Health and Social Services Departments, Juvenile Court, Mental Health Association, N.C. Congress of Parents and Teachers, Welfare Councils, N.C. Department of Public Instructions, Vocational Rehabilitation, students, citizens, and expert consultants. Committees organized on specific problem areas could hammer out such specifics as architectural design of the center, selection of staff, content of service, and training and research programs. This approach would set in motion a high and positive image and visibility of the Division of Youth Services in North Carolina.

Innovation in Juvenile Delinquency

Development and implementation of:

- Specialized treatment, rehabilitation, and education programs for very young delinquent children to understand prevention as well as remediation to delinquency.
- To tap all available resources in the Triangle area to support a coordinate system of prevention and services.
- To train personnel, both inservice and preservice, in a variety of disciplines and at various levels for:
  - *Training schools throughout the State*
  - *Public schools*
  - *Community-based programs*
- To develop research and evaluation strategies to lead us to better approaches in assisting this kind of troubled child.
- Transport all need findings and approaches to schools, communities, and institutions of higher education. Since there is no precedent for this program; i.e., no other state has so far attempted this type of program, it could be a national model for the treatment, rehabilitation, and education of young delinquent children.

Cost Factors

This program proposal could be defended in terms of costs by planning to take the youngest children out of existing programs and move them to the center, move older delinquent children to both community-based programs and other training schools, and close out one or two of existing training schools.

The most qualified, experienced, and notably successful staff throughout the training schools in North Carolina could be transferred to this center. Staff from the other training schools could be required to attend training modules periodically at the proposed center for further training and upgrading.

All of the above issues and many more could justify the cost factors relative to the development of this center.

There will no doubt that federal funding would be assured from the various federal agencies relative to this development in view of the innovativeness and futuristic program components.

Possible Associated Innovations Tangent to Development of Proposed Center

Joint program development to be associated with the proposed center would be an Institute for the Study of Child Advocacy. Since North Carolina is the first state to institute child advocacy procedures in its training schools, it would be plausible for the Division of Youth Services to consider the possibility to associate with this proposal an organization unit to study child advocacy, to train child advocates, and research the potential of child advocacy as a viable approach to help children. The Institute for the Study of Child Advocacy would work cooperatively with the Governor's Advocacy Council and all other facets of the advocacy movement in state, public, and private sectors. This would be another "first" for North Carolina.

The implementation of the proposed program could serve as a national model and/or laboratory for the service of young delinquent and/or adjudicated boys and girls.

The proposed center could provide workshops and seminars for the courts, judges, and counselors relative to the needs of children.

There has been no major breakthrough in research relative to the competencies necessary for personnel serving delinquent young children. Subsequently, there is no single training program where professional consensus of opinion agrees that potential and existing professionals in this field can go for quality training.

Summary

Generally, personnel in correctional programs for children and youth responsible for troubled children have not been trained in specific preparation programs for disturbed or behavioral disordered, delinquent children in special education, behavioral management or modification, child development, mental health, psychiatric social work, and so forth. If services for children and youth are viewed as a priority, training resources must reflect this commitment. A new century, 2000, ought to bring with it futuristic and thoughtful government planning for these difficult children and youth.

Chapter Seventeen

Delivery of Services Model: Boards for Children in Trouble

All the so-called revitalizing in American public education to assure the proper implementation of appropriate educational and mental health programs to produce an adjusted, educated citizenry will fail unless the power structure of local, state, or federal/national groups that are organized and educationally oriented have a structured role and function in creating the best education and socialization programs in the nation's schools for troubled children.

We must begin early intervention by reaching the child who is troubled in his or her own home long before the beginning of formal schooling. In this approach, the school may succeed in intervening early enough to influence the learning climate in the home, where the most influential behavior patterning takes place. Instruction outside the school building may be necessary to help some children who are disturbed or troubled to maintain pace with their peers. The school-sponsored programs could reach these children through such channels as community school agencies, neighborhood services, church programs, job training, pediatric services, and mental health centers. As the schools find ways to make their programs less institution bound and communicate something of value to children who are disturbed regardless of time and place, they will come closer to a position of centrality in community life.

In this context, we suggest the establishment of parent and child centers to service communities in the earliest interventions; provide elaborate school readiness services and school orientation for parents, pressing for achievement in the home; and finally establish the position of child development specialists and services in the school.

The chief vehicle to achieve this reorientation is the creation of Boards for Children in Trouble. The Boards could then reach aggressively into the community: sending workers out to children's homes, recreational facilities, and schools; developing new services; contracting for others; and modifying existing agencies so that the range of needs discovered is matched by the range of services available. They should assume full responsibility for all education in the community that is peripheral to schooling, including preprimary education, parent education, and community education. They should take steps to ensure parity in planning and decision making on the part of all relevant publics.

These Boards for Children in Trouble should be organized around individual schools. The schools would then become, under the auspices of these Boards, wide-ranging developmental centers bringing to bear agency and community resources and using professionals from a variety of disciplines and professional systems in a total developmental program for children in trouble.

Special education personnel should be responsible for assuring that all children benefit from highly specialized and general education programs. In the schools, the mental health needs of the organization and the training needs of teachers and the school staff become a primary focus. The test here, however, relates to the children in trouble and their teachers and not to the needs of the school. Teachers should not seek out special educational services to help them end up with the students they wish they had, rather than the ones who are there for them to teach.

Too often, children in trouble are the losers because the necessary services are nonexistent or overcrowded if available, adding to the problems children must overcome. An effective Board for Children in Trouble would clarify the problems on the basis of child needs, and our sophisticated research and development can then be brought to bear—uncomplicated by a myriad of social variable and failures—on questions related to the developmental needs of highly divergent children (Tompkins & McGill, 1989).

Challenge To The Future

The profession of working with children who are troubled as it now exists has several needs. Basic among these is the need for planning and programming. The nature of children's needs must be identified. Necessary and appropriate resources must be determined. Ongoing children's programs can be used, and cooperation among them must be developed. New services are not proposed immediately, but there must be better planning of existing services. There is the need for development of new ideas, improvements of present arrangements, inventions of methods of intervention, and ways of coordinating services and agencies.

Another need is for continuing evaluation of children's services. This means not only studying the effectiveness of programs and services but also developing the capability to know the resources of the community, the way they work together, and the degree they utilize the best in current practices and knowledge about children's services.

Finally, there is the need to assure the legal rights of children. Children have a right to adequate living arrangements, food, clothing, education, medical attention, and the like. In light of these concerns, we should view and define advocacy as the process of constructing programs connecting children to appropriate programs.

Summary

The implications are:

- Provision of adequate services for children.
- Development of community responsiveness, responsibility, and accountability to and for children.
- Involvement of both public and private resources to assist children.
- Development of program standards.

The challenge is that it is more difficult to find a solution to fit the child than to fit the child to the solution. The challenge is to create engineering capacities to help child-serving agencies to reassess policies, standards, procedures, and practices and to hold us and them accountable for sustaining appropriate goals and programs on the basis of children's needs.

The challenge is to attract individual and groups of parents, citizens, and professionals at all levels to pick up the gauntlet on behalf of children....

Source: J.R. Tompkins (1996). Special education movement in the education of students who are seriously emotionally disturbed. Motto: Move as slowly as you can. In B. Brooks and D. Sabatino (Eds.), *Personal perspectives on emotional disturbance/behavioral disorders*, (pp. 368–371). Austin, TX: PRO-ED. Reprinted with permission.

References

Biklen, D. (1976). Advocacy comes of age. *Exceptional Children, 52*, 308–313.

Child Advocacy Commission of Durham (1997). *Child Advocacy*, Durham, NC: Child Advocacy Commission of Durham, Inc., 1–3.

Forness, S.R. (1997). Personal reflections: Definition. In James Kauffman (author). *Characteristics of emotional and behavioral disorders of children and youth*, (p. 36). Columbus, OH: Merrill/Prentice Hall.

Frith, G.H. (1981). "Advocates" vs. "professional employee": A question of priorities for special educators. *Exceptional Children, 47*, 486–492.

Hewett, F.M. (1987). The ecological view of disturbed children: Shadow versus substance. *The Pointer, 31* (3), 61–63.

Hines, M.L. (1987). *Don't get mad: Get powerful! A manual for building advocacy skills.* Lansing, MI: Michigan Protection and Advocacy Service.

Hobbs, N. (1975). *The futures of children: Categories, labels, and their consequences.* San Francisco, CA: Jossey-Bass Publishers, pp. 161, 185–188.

Joint Commission on Mental Health of Children. (1970). *Crisis in child mental health: Challenge for the 1970's.* New York, NY: Harper & Row, 6, 17, 185, 376.

Kahn, A.J., Kamerman, S.B., & McGowan, B.G. (1972). *Child advocacy: A report of a national baseline study.* New York, NY:

Columbia University School of Social Work and A Child Advocacy Research Project, 41–42.

Lewis, W.L. (1970). Child advocacy and ecological planning. *Mental Hygiene, 54* (4), 475–483.

Lourie, Norman, V. (Spring, 1972). The question of advocacy: The many forces of advocacy. *Public Welfare, 30* (2), 12–15.

McGregor, D.L., Petzel, B.B., Jones, P.R., McCoun, P.J., & Cole, R.L. (1982). Readers respond: The advocacy dilemma. *Exceptional Children, 49*, 14–17.

McLauglin, J.A. (1995). Research as a tool for advocacy: A commentary. *Remedial and Special Education, 16* (4), 195–198.

Morgan, S.R. (1985). *Children in crisis: A team approach in the schools.* San Diego, CA: College-Hill Press.

Moynihan, D.P. (1993). Defining deviance down. *The American Scholar, 62*, 17–30.

National Mental Health Association and The Federation of Families for Children's Mental Health (1993). *All systems failure: An examination of the results of neglecting the needs of children with serious emotional disturbance.* Washington, DC: National Mental Health Association.

North Carolina Department of Public Instruction: N.C. Department of Student Information Management Certified Head Count for Special Education (1992). Raleigh, NC: NCDPI.

Paul, James L. (1977). A framework for understanding advocacy. In J.L. Paul, G.R. Neufeld, and J.W. Pelosi (Eds.), (pp. 11–31), Syracuse, NY: Syracuse University Press.

Paul, J.L., Stedman, D.J., & Neufeld, G.N. (1977) (Eds.), (pp. 269–270), *De-institutionalization: Program and policy development.* Syracuse, NY: Syracuse University Press.

Paul, J.L., Pelosi, J.W., & Ray, R.S. (1976). *Child Advocacy System Project.* Durham, NC: Learning Institute of North Carolina.

Paul, J.L., & Pelosi, J.W. (1971). *Child advocacy systems project.* Durham, NC: The Learning Institute of North Carolina (LINC).

Pelosi, J. (1971). *A multi-year development of child advocacy system.* Durham, NC: Learning Institute of North Carolina (LINC), 10–12.

Reay, W. (February, 1996). The rise of the unworthy. *Claiming Children.* Alexandria, VA: Federation of Families for Children's Mental Health.

Renzulli, J.S., & Reis, S.M. (1991). Building advocacy through program design, student productivity and public relations. *Gifted Child Quarterly, 35* (4), 182–187.

Rhodes, W.C. (1970). A community participation analysis for emotionally disturbed children. *Exceptional Children, 37,* 309–314.

Rhodes, W.C. (1967). The disturbing child: A problem of ecological management. *Exceptional Children,* 33 (7), 449–455.

Rock, S.L., Geiger, W.L., & Hood, G. (1992). CEC's standards for professional practice in advocacy: Members' attitudes and activities. *Exceptional Children, 58* (6), 541–547.

Sarason, S.B. (1990). *The predictable failure of educational reform: Can we change course before it's too late?* San Francisco, CA: Jossey-Bass Publishers.

Smith, C.R. (1997). Advocacy for students with emotional and behavior disorders: One call for redirected efforts. *Behavioral Disorders, 22* (2), 96–105.

State of North Carolina Study Commission for Emotionally Disturbed Children (1970). *Report of the task force on child advocacy,* Raleigh, NC: N.C. Department of Mental Health.

Tompkins, J.R. (1996). Special education movement in the education of students who are seriously emotionally disturbed. Motto: Move as slowly as you can. In B. Brooks and D. Sabatino (Eds.), *Personal perspectives on emotional disturbance/behavioral disorders.* (pp. 368–371). Austin, TX: PRO-ED.

Tompkins, J.R., & McGill, P.L. (1989). Lack of educational and treatment services for students in trouble: A new proposal for help. *The Pointer, 33* (3), 38–42.

Tompkins, J.R., & McGill, P.L. (1993). *Surviving in schools in the 1990's: Strategic Management of School Environments.* Lanham, MD: University Press of America.

Tompkins, J.R., & Stahl, R. (Summer 1976). Teacher Preparation for Gifted Children, *North Carolina Association for Gifted and Talented Quarterly Journal.*

Tompkins, J.R. "Child Advocacy," (September 1997). In Judith E. Goldstein (Ed.), *Consultation: Enhancing Leisure Service Delivery to Handicapped Children and Youth.* (pp. 45–49). Washington, DC: National Recreation and Park Association.

Tompkins, J., Brooks, B., & Dorne, W. (Spring Issue, 1977). Child Advocacy: A Parent Training Approach. *Eastern Illinois State University Educational Journal. X,* (2).

Tracey, M., & Gibbins, M. (1971). Education. (Contributors on sections Establish Advocacy Programs, Special Education Neglected). *Report of The White House Conference on Youth.* Washington, DC: U.S. Government Printing Office, (Stock No. 4000-0267), 97–99.

White House Conference on Children. *Report to the President.* Washington, DC: U.S. Government Printing Office, (Stock No. 4000-0267), 91–92, 99, 179, 283.

Wolfensberger, Wolf. (1972). *Citizen advocacy Toronto: National Institute of Mental Retardation.*

Wolfensberger, Wolf. (1971). Toward citizen advocacy for the handicapped. Lincoln, NB: Nebraska Psychiatric Institute, University of Nebraska Medical Center.

Wolfensberger, W. (1971a). Will there always be an institution?: The impact of epidemiological trends. *Mental Retardation, 9* (5), 14–20.

Wolfensberger, W. (1971b). Will there always be an institution?: Residential alternatives to institutions. *Mental Retardation, 9* (6), 31–38.

Wolfensberger, W. (1971c). Child advocacy perspectives. Unpublished paper, Washington, DC: Joint Commission on Mental Health of Children and U.S. Department of Health, Education, & Welfare.

Wolfensberger, W. (1969). The origin and nature of our institutional models. In R.B. Kugel and W. Wolfensberger (Eds.). (pp. 71–78*). Changing patterns of residential services for the mentally retarded.* Washington, DC: President's Committee on Mental Retardation.

Wolfensberger, W. (1969). Twenty predictions about the future of residential services in mental retardation. *Mental Retardation, 7* (6), 51–54.

About the Authors

James R. Tompkins

James Tompkins received his Ph.D. in educational psychology from Catholic University of America in 1971. He was coordinator of the Unit of Education of Emotionally Disturbed Children, Division of Training Programs, Bureau for the Education of the Handicapped in Washington, D.C. from 1965-1971. He has served as the Director of the Governor's Child Advocacy Council in North Carolina and as an adjunct professor at the University of North Carolina-Chapel Hill. Dr. Tompkins also has worked as a consultant in public and parochial elementary schools and in residential treatment of children who were emotionally behavioral disordered. He currently is a professor of special education in the area of emotional-behavioral disorders at Appalachian State University. Dr. Tompkins recently co-authored a text on the use of milieu therapy "Surviving in the Schools in the 1990's: Strategic Management of School Environments."

Benjamin L. Brooks

Benjamin Brooks is currently Director, Center for the Advancement of Exceptional Children's Services, Belmont Abbey College, Belmont Abbey, North Carolina and professor of special education. Dr. Brooks has taught both special and regular education and has been an administrator of program in higher education for more than 20 years. In addition to public school and university teaching, he directed an adolescent and children's program in a private psychiatric hospital for three years. Dr. Brooks has been and continues to be a strong advocate for children with disabilities. He has represented parents in due process hearings in three different states. Dr. Brooks also has authored handbooks for due process hearing and prepared workshops for parents to enlighten them as to their legal status under the Individuals with Disabilities Education Act (IDEA).

Timothy J. Tompkins

Tim Tompkins graduated with a Master Degree in Public Affairs from the L.B.J. School of Public Affairs at the University of Texas at Austin in 1990. After graduation, Tim served as a Legislative Aide for United States Senator Terry Sanford. He spent a number of years working as Director of Community Relations for various non-profit organizations and managed the campaign for United States Congressman David Price in 1994. His community activities include serving as President of the Board of the Durham City Child Advocacy Commission, North Carolina, and Vice President of the Board for the Triangle Residential Options for Substance Abusers. He is a graduate of the North Carolina Institute of Political Leadership, and Durham Chamber of Commerce Leadership Program. He recently served as part of a delegation to Mexico with the American Council of Young Political Leaders, and a five-week Rotary delegation to Denmark. He also hosts a cable television program that examines various public policy issues, and has co-authored several publications on the education and treatment of emotionally disturbed children. Mr. Tompkins is currently Community Relations Manager, City Search, Morrisville, North Carolina.